Best Practices for Therapy

Empirically Based Treatment Protocols

Dear Mental Health Professional:

This protocol is part of the *Best Practices for Therapy* that is designed to provide mental health practitioners empirically based treatment programs. We have edited this series to be clear and user-friendly, yet comprehensive and step-by-step.

The series offers high quality, consistently formatted protocols that include everything you need to initiate and complete treatment. Each session is outlined in detail with its own agenda, client education materials, and skill-building interventions. Each session also provides sample instructions and therapist-client dialogues.

The therapist protocol you are using corresponds with an available client manual that is designed to be used concurrently. Your protocol has all the worksheets, homework assignments, in-session treatment exercises, and didactic material that is in the client manual. Also included are pre- and post-assessments, and an overall program evaluation. An appendix contains a treatment plan summary (now required by many managed care companies).

Ten *Best Practices for Therapy* protocols are currently available or in development. They include protocols for PTSD, GAD, OCD, panic disorde/agoraphobiar, specific phobia, social phobia, depression, anger management, BPD, and eating disorders.

We wish you every success in using this program with your clients.

Sincerely,

Matthew McKay, Ph.D.
John Preston, Psy.D.
Carole Honeychurch, M.A.

OVERCOMING PANIC DISORDER AND AGORAPHOBIA

■

A Cognitive Restructuring
and Exposure-Based Protocol
for the Treatment of Panic
and Agoraphobia

Elke Zuercher-White, Ph.D.

BPT

Best Practices for Therapy
Empirically Based Treatment Protocols

Questionnaire on page 28 Copyright 1990 George A. Clum, Publisher, Blacksburg, Va. 24060; ISBN No. 0-534-11295-1

Distributed in the U.S.A. by Publishers Group West; in Canada by Raincoast Books; in Great Britain by Airlift Book Company, Ltd.; in South Africa by Real Books, Ltd.; in Australia by Boobook; and in New Zealand by Tandem Press.

Copyright © 1999 by Elke Zuercher-White, Ph.D.
New Harbinger Publications, Inc.
5674 Shattuck Avenue
Oakland, CA 94609

Cover design by Poulson/Gluck Design
Edited by Carole Honeychurch
Text design by Michele Waters

ISBN 1-57224-146-2 Paperback

New Harbinger Publications' Website address: www.newharbinger.com

01   00   99

10   9   8   7   6   5   4   3   2   1

First printing

Contents

Introduction

Overview of the Disorder

Individuals with panic disorder are more likely to seek help than those with many other emotional problems, including other anxiety disorders. However, they often seek help in medical settings (primary care physicians and hospital emergency rooms) rather than mental health clinics (Katerndahl and Realini 1995). This is related to the nature of the disorder, which includes a number of physical symptoms. The person believes that something is physically wrong with him or her. The complaints are often cardiovascular, gastrointestinal, and neurologic (Katon 1989). Although it is appropriate for the physician to examine the client to rule out a medical condition with symptoms that mimic panic attacks, the extensive tests that are sometimes performed may frighten the individual further. In the absence of a disease, the disorder is often not correctly diagnosed. Too often the client is told it is stress and sent home with a few tranquilizers or low-dose antidepressants, often constituting the only treatment they get. Clients who are not convinced by the explanation about the origin of their symptoms or believe that they are not taken seriously are likely to seek help in yet another medical office, losing precious time.

The client who is correctly diagnosed and referred to a mental-health professional competent to treat this disorder is more fortunate. Especially when the client presents in the early stages of the disorder, he or she is usually more easily treatable. This is particularly the case if fear has not yet taken a strong hold, and agoraphobia, a further complication of panic disorder, has not developed. Although, as with any disorder, the sooner the client is properly diagnosed and treated, the better; short delays in panic disorder can rapidly lead to very dramatic deterioration.

Major Clinical Features

Panic attacks are described as overwhelming experiences, consisting of a number of frightening symptoms. When you probe into the client's fear, "catastrophic" cognitions are often verbalized. The fears are physical in nature, e.g., the fear of having a heart attack, a stroke, or fainting. Other fears are mental or behavioral—the client fears becoming insane or losing control. As fear takes its hold, many people start avoiding situations where they fear having panics, like driving on the freeway or going to stores and malls.

Identifying Panic Attacks

Before diagnosing panic disorder, the clinician must determine the presence of panic attacks. The *DSM-IV* (American Psychiatric Association 1994) defines panic attacks as sudden episodes of intense fear or anxiety, and consisting of a number of physical and cognitive symptoms. The attacks must peak within ten minutes and include at least four of the following thirteen symptoms:

Panic Attack Symptoms*

(1) palpitations, pounding heart, or accelerated heart rate

(2) sweating

(3) trembling or shaking

(4) sensations of shortness of breath or smothering

(5) feeling of choking

(6) chest pain or discomfort

(7) nausea or abdominal distress

(8) feeling dizzy, unsteady, lightheaded, or faint

(9) derealization (feelings of unreality) or depersonalization (being detached from oneself)

(10) fear of losing control or going crazy

(11) fear of dying

(12) paresthesias (numbness or tingling sensations)

(13) chills or hot flushes

Fewer than four symptoms are called limited symptom attacks and do not constitute full-blown panic attacks. As the client improves in treatment, there are often limited symptom attacks on the way to recovery. If the symptoms take longer than ten minutes to reach a peak, it is high anxiety but not panic "attacks," which by definition occur suddenly.

---

* Reprinted with permission from the *Diagnostic and Statistical Manual of Mental Disorders*, Fourth Edition. Copyright 1994 American Psychiatric Association.

Diagnosis

In panic disorder, some panic attacks occur unexpectedly, i.e., not only in specific contexts. There is a great deal of variability within and between individuals as far as the panic symptoms, where the panics occur, and whether they are expected or unexpected. Panic attacks that are expected and occur in certain situations (often while driving) are often more severe and intense than spontaneous, unexpected panic attacks (e.g., occurring at home) (Dijkman-Caes, Kraan, and deVries 1993).

Panic Disorder: For the *DSM-IV* diagnosis of panic disorder, the person must have had at least two recurrent, unexpected panic attacks, *or* one attack followed by at least one month of persistent fear about having another attack, worry about the consequences of the attacks, or significant behavioral change as a result of the attacks (such as avoidance, visits to the emergency room, etc.). The attacks must not occur in response to illegal drugs, medications, or physical illness. As the disorder progresses, there is a greater likelihood that the person develops chronic anxiety and worry not necessarily related to having another panic.

Agoraphobia: Many people start to avoid situations because it seems natural to do when afraid. It becomes their coping mechanism. Agoraphobia develops in these instances as a consequence—a complication of panic disorder. Hence, there is panic disorder without agoraphobia (300.01) and panic disorder with agoraphobia (300.21). *Agoraphobia* is the fear of being in places or situations where, in case of a panic, it is difficult to escape because of physical or social constraints or because help is not immediately available. Typical agoraphobic situations are: driving, going to stores and malls, using public transportation, going to restaurants and parties, standing in line, using elevators, and so on. The avoidance can range from mild, with little interference with the person's functioning, to the extreme of keeping the person housebound. It should be noted, however, that the relationship between panic and agoraphobia remains complex and not fully understood. Often, phobias were present prior to the first panic. The implication is that the person already has learned to respond to anxiety with avoidance.

Agoraphobia Without History of Panic Disorder: In agoraphobia without history of panic disorder (300.22) the person has never fully met the criteria for panic disorder. Yet there is often a fear of acute bursts of panic-like symptoms or limited symptom attacks (Goisman, Warshaw, Steketee, et al. 1995). The person may feel incapacitated by the fear of loss of bladder or bowel control, vomiting, fainting, or otherwise losing control of their behavior. The need for clarification of no prior history of panic disorder arises because many clients with panic disorder and a pervasive avoidance pattern may *no longer* have uncued panic attacks (coming out of the blue), experiencing attacks only in the context of the avoided feared situations. In these latter cases, the diagnosis is panic disorder with agoraphobia.

As the concept of panic disorder has become more widely known, a number of false positives are observed: clients who claim to have panic attacks but do not have them. Some of them experience high anxiety and label these episodes as panic attacks. Others have panic attacks but not panic disorder. The widespread occurrence of panic attacks makes it particularly important to learn to diagnose the disorder correctly.

In the clinical setting, you often see clients who do not have just panic disorder. Other comorbid Axis I diagnoses and/or personality disorders complicate the picture. The rigors of cognitive-behavior therapy (CBT) for panic disorder may make it too difficult for a person who is, for instance, severely depressed to attend to the treatment protocol. It may behoove the client to have the depression treated first, at least until they are able to function again.

Prevalence

Panic attacks are a common phenomenon. Barlow (1988) reviewed and reported studies showing that the occurrence of panic attacks in the general population within the previous year was about 35 percent. This means that lifetime prevalences are higher. However, only a small proportion develop panic disorder.

Panic disorder with and without agoraphobia is for many a debilitating condition, and it afflicts one out of every seventy-five people in their lifetime (Treatment of Panic Disorder 1991). According to the National Comorbidity Survey (Kessler, McGonagle, Zhao, et al. 1994), panic disorder occurs in 3.5 percent and agoraphobia without panic disorder in 5.3 percent of the population. As mentioned earlier, many individuals with panic disorder seek care in medical settings. Fortunately, physicians are becoming more knowledgeable about this condition and adept at recognizing it. In 1990 people suffering with panic disorder were referred significantly more often for psychiatric consultation compared to 1980 (Gerdes, Yates, and Clancy 1995).

While most people coming to mental health clinics present with panic disorder with agoraphobia, it is ideal to identify and treat also those with a recent onset of panic disorder, in many cases before agoraphobia has set in. Clients in the early stages of the disorder are more treatable and have a better prognosis than those with long-term panic disorder and agoraphobia.

Treatment Approach

The National Institutes of Health (NIH) *Consensus Statement* (Treatment of Panic Disorder 1991) states that two treatments are effective in panic disorder: cognitive-behavior therapy and medications (antidepressants and high-potency benzodiazepines). Their efficacy has been substantiated with a great deal of research. Although other treatments (such as psychodynamic) may help a number of clients, the results are seldom achieved consistently within a brief therapy format (fewer than twenty sessions).

Just as with medications, there is not one single cognitive-behavior therapy model for panic disorder. Among the variations are models that heavily emphasize behavioral interventions, others cognitive, while yet others combine both types of interventions. The treatment described here consists of cognitive and behavioral approaches, largely based on David Barlow's inclusive model, which integrates the two.

Conceptualization Behind This Approach

Panic disorder has biological and psychological determinants and a current stressor often brings on the first panic. Biological factors include the possibility that in some individuals there is an increased propensity for different dysregulations, sometimes genetically determined. Some of the more prevalent theories are: There is a heightened vulnerability to anxiety; the fight/flight response is elicited more easily; there is an increased carbon dioxide sensitivity and as a consequence the suffocation alarm is being elicited more readily; the person hyperventilates chronically; there are audiovestibular dysfunctions; or, a dysregulation of the noradrenergic, the benzodiazepine, or the serotonin systems can be deducted (Barlow 1988; Clark, Hirsch, Smith, et al. 1994; Hoffman, O'Leary, and Munjack 1994; Ley 1985, 1988; Klein 1993; Margraf, Ehlers, and Roth 1986; McNally 1994).

Psychological theories consist of various fear theories (Barlow 1988; Williams 1987); cognitive models about the structure and maintenance of fear (Beck and Emery, with Greenberg 1985; Clark 1986; Clark and Ehlers 1993; Foa and Kozak 1986); self-efficacy theory (Bandura 1977, 1988; Williams 1992); anxiety sensitivity (Reiss 1987; Reiss, Peterson, Gursky, and McNally 1986; McNally 1990, 1994); and psychodynamic theories (Fyer, Mannuzza, and Coplan 1995).

Barlow's biopsychosocial model of panic explains the process from a panic attack to panic disorder (Barlow 1986, 1988, 1997). Anxiety and the fight/flight response are present in us humans and all species with a sensory system and the ability to move. This response allows the organism to attempt to survive a perceived threat. Barlow labels the fear reaction that occurs in response to an imminently life-threatening event a "true alarm." The same reaction occurring in the absence of a real threat is a "false alarm" or panic attack. Either a "true" or a "false alarm" may lead to "learned alarms," i.e., the person learns to repeatedly respond to a specific stimulus with fear. This could occur as a result of biological preparedness, conditioning, generalization, and/or catastrophic misinterpretations. (An example of a "true alarm" becoming a "learned alarm" is when a person is unable to drive on the freeway following a bad car accident. While such an avoidance is common for a short time as the result of the traumatic experience, in some cases the fear and avoidance do not remit.)

According to Barlow, in panic disorder the person learns to expect with dread the recurrence of the fear response (the panic attack) itself, and the anticipation leads to a state of anxious apprehension. This happens in particular if the attacks are experienced as unpredictable and uncontrollable. As a result of the apprehension over further panics, the person becomes exquisitely vigilant to the recurrence of such symptoms. This increases arousal and perpetuates the fear cycle. Fear cognitions and hypersensitivity to dreaded somatic sensations develop.

The treatment then aims to eliminate the fear of panic attacks. This is accomplished through cognitive means to repudiate the misinterpretations and through behavioral means to diminish the exaggerated emotional reactivity. One would logically hope that once panic fear is eradicated, phobic fears would as a consequence vanish. This is not the case. Exposure to the feared situation is required to achieve habituation and confidence in confronting it.

Basic Elements of Cognitive-Behavior Therapy for Panic Disorder

Psychoeducation

This component gives the client an understanding of the nature of anxiety and panic attacks: normalizing anxiety, learning about the fight/flight response and its physiology, and the connection between panic and the fight/flight response. The panic attack is viewed as a response, a process comprising physiological, cognitive, and behavioral manifestations.

Breathing Retraining: Diaphragmatic Breathing

Since a number of clients with panic disorder are chronic hyperventilators and many panic attacks are accompanied by acute hyperventilation, learning to apply slow, diaphragmatic breathing allows the person to stop hyperventilation. Furthermore, it helps slow down other panic symptoms. Diaphragmatic breathing is an effective coping mechanism, which many clients find exceedingly useful when confronting feared physical symptoms and feared situations.

Cognitive Restructuring

This component addresses the erroneous thoughts concerning the dangerousness of the panic symptoms. The goal of cognitive restructuring is to modify the automatic thoughts that reflect the misinterpretations. The process used to achieve this is collaborative empiricism and Socratic dialogue. You guide your client to view the negative thoughts as hypotheses, and together you challenge these hypotheses. Verbal inductive techniques involve posing a series of questions that help the client challenge his or her own thinking and arrive at a different conclusion. Behavioral experiments are often employed as well to test the validity and survivability of the original assumptions held by the client. This is very different from using the therapist's authoritative knowledge to convince the person or having the client repeat positive self-statements.

At a deeper level, core beliefs can be explored which support the negative, catastrophic automatic thoughts. This allows for more profound change beyond the simple elimination of panic attacks and amelioration of panic disorder.

Interoceptive Exposure

This is a behavioral way of confronting the fears in panic disorder. It is based on the hypothesis that the person has also become conditioned to respond with fear to certain sensations. The client engages in a series of exercises designed to bring on symptoms similar to the ones in panic. Through repetition deconditioning from the feared sensations is achieved, not unlike the deconditioning from fear in phobic situations, which is achieved through repeated *in vivo* exposure.

In Vivo Exposure in Agoraphobia

Cognitive shifts do not automatically result in elimination of phobic fear, hence, the fear has to be addressed separately. *In vivo* exposure involves stepwise, frequent, and prolonged exposures to feared situations. To achieve mastery over the fear, the client must refrain from using protective signals or behaviors designed to save them from a catastrophe.

Adjuncts to Success and Relapse Prevention

I have found other elements important in the treatment of panic disorder: teaching clients strategies to deal more effectively with chronic worry, assertiveness training, and especially in new panickers, helping them resolve crises that often precipitated the onset of panics.

Relapse prevention is a crucial part of the treatment. The therapist prepares the client for a return of symptoms and helps him or her find ways to avoid connecting them with fear anew. The best deterrents to relapse are maintaining the new behaviors and the present-focused cognitive style that were learned in therapy.

Research

The efficacy of CBT has been shown in a number of studies. Barlow and colleagues (Barlow 1990; Barlow, Craske, Cerny, et al. 1989; Craske 1991; Craske, Brown, and Barlow 1991; Klosko, Barlow, Tassinari, et al. 1990) demonstrated that their panic control treatment (PCT), which included interoceptive exposure and cognitive therapy, was significantly superior to placebo and wait list. About 85 percent of the clients in the PCT group became panic-free. At two years' follow-up, 81.3 percent of the PCT group, 42.9 percent of the PCT plus relaxation group, and 35.7 percent of the relaxation group were panic-free. Hence, adding relaxation to their protocol diminished the results over time. Although the PCT group did better than another group receiving alprazolam (Xanax), the results were not significant. However, the alprazolam group did not do significantly better than the placebo group. In contrast, the PCT group did significantly better than placebo.

Clark, Salkovskis, Hackmann, et al. (1994) compared cognitive therapy (including behavioral techniques) to applied relaxation and imipramine. Although clients from all three treatment conditions improved significantly over those on wait list, the cognitive therapy group was significantly more effective on a number of panic and anxiety measures and less likely to relapse fifteen months later than was the imipramine group. In all the studies mentioned above, clients had no, mild, or moderate agoraphobia.

Marks, Swinson, Basoglu, et al. (1993) studied panic disorder with agoraphobia. They compared the following treatment conditions: alprazolam and exposure, alprazolam and relaxation, placebo and exposure, and placebo and relaxation for eight weeks. They were followed for up to forty-three weeks. When looking at the panic measures, all groups improved. In phobias, mood, and general disability, exposure and alprazolam were effective, but exposure was twice as effective as alprazolam. Only the subjects in the exposure group maintained their gains at follow-up.

Another study on panic disorder and agoraphobia showed significant results in the cognitive therapy group compared to supportive psychotherapy, with gains maintained at one-year follow-up (Beck, Sokol, Clark, et al. 1992). Marchione, Michelson, Greenwald, et al. (1987) found that therapist-directed graduated exposure with cognitive restructuring or progressive relaxation was more effective than exposure alone. This treatment was conducted in groups.

Studies from various countries show that over 80 percent achieve panic-free states after short-term CBT, which are maintained one to two years later (Clark and Ehlers 1993; Margraf, Barlow, Clark, et al. 1993; Michelson and Marchione 1991). Improvement is also achieved in general anxiety, agoraphobia, anticipatory anxiety, and depression. The consensus is that integrated, multimodal treatments are most effective, i.e., those encompassing the components listed earlier (Gould, Otto, and Pollack 1995; van den Hout, Arntz, and Hoekstra 1994; Lidren, Watkins, Gould, et al. 1994; Telch, Schmidt, Jaimez, et al. 1995).

Duration of Treatment

Treatment of panic disorder takes from ten to sixteen sessions; fifteen is often reported in the literature (Gould, Otto, and Pollock 1995). About twelve sessions are often sufficient in panic disorder without agoraphobia; sixteen sessions are often needed for panic disorder with agoraphobia. Treatment sessions are usually conducted once a week.

If only eight sessions are provided (e.g., when limits are posed by a managed care company), you can teach the client the physiology of panic and hyperventilation, diaphragmatic breathing, how to use thought records, do interoceptive exposures, and set up agoraphobic exposures. You would not have the same opportunity to follow through with the entire treatment, provide guidance and support, and help when the client gets "stuck" as you would in the longer treatment mentioned here. Research into even shorter treatments is being conducted.

Assessment

The first meeting with your client is crucial. It allows for sharing of information, establishes how you work, and provides an opportunity to build an alliance with him or her. Specifically, you will ask questions that are required to make a definitive diagnosis, assess urgent conditions and health problems, and explore cultural differences. You will assess whether modifications in the treatment are in order as a result of the information you gathered. Then you can share your treatment strategies, appraise the client's overall goals and motivation, and instill hope.

The key diagnostic issue is to establish the presence of panic attacks and to determine if the *DSM-IV* criteria for panic disorder and agoraphobia are met. When and under what circumstances did the symptoms begin? If some time ago, how has the disorder progressed over time? This takes you into precipitants and a brief history of the disorder. Further, you need information to differentiate panic disorder from other conditions. Are there other anxiety disorders, depression, or chemical dependence (substance abuse)? Even though other disorders exist, will they interfere with treatment? Does the client need to see a physician to rule out health problems? A medical condition does not preclude the client from having emotional problems; in fact, they may exacerbate each other. You need to assess the overall severity of the client's condition. Does the client need a medication referral to a psychiatrist?

The suspicion of a physical condition or finding of other emotional problems may take you to a decision tree: What needs to be attended to first? It is very rare that I have met a client with panic disorder who is suicidal. There are clients with a concomitant severe depression who might reveal suicidal ideation, if asked. Nothing takes precedence over attending to such safety issues. If a physical exam seems to be in order, a referral should be made. Although a health problem may only be found on occasion, it behooves you to stay alert to that possibility.

Will other conditions likely interfere with the panic and phobia work? Three common conditions are substance abuse, depression, and post-traumatic stress disorder. Almost invariably, *substance abuse must be brought under control first.* Once under control, you can work with anxiety problems, provided that your client remains in substance-abuse treatment. If depression is *secondary* to the anxiety problem, the panic protocol is usually indicated. On the other hand, you might find that there is primary depression, and it is severe enough that the client cannot attend to the task at hand. Remember that CBT for panic and phobia disorders is quite rigorous. Sometimes panic and phobias result from a traumatic experience that has not been addressed. By having your client deal with the ramifications of the trauma first, you are validating the client's experience and, as he or she masters it, many anxiety symptoms tend to remit. Is there a personality disorder? It may not become apparent in the assessment but show up later. Most often you can treat the client who has a personality disorder. Other times personality disorders may be severe enough so that gains made in this treatment modality are limited.

In order to accomplish all of the above, you need to stay very focused. You want to have enough information to formulate the case. Extensive history taking is usually not necessary and would easily extend the evaluation beyond one session. If the client feels that you are competent, understanding, and interested in helping him or her overcome the problems, it is likely that you will develop a good working alliance.

Patient Self-Rating Scales

Three basic measures are in order when treating panic disorder: 1) An ongoing rating of frequency and severity of panics 2), a measure of the fear of panics, and 3) in agoraphobia, a measure of the confidence in approaching feared situations. (The best measure of agoraphobic avoidance is naturally an observation of actual behavior, but this is time consuming and thus difficult to apply in traditional clinical settings.) The following measures will help assess progress in each of these catagories over time. (You will find them in the assessment chapter.)

1. Worksheet 1: Panic Frequency and Intensity is to be filled out by the client daily. It is thus an ongoing measure.

2. The Panic Attack Cognitions Questionnaire (PACQ) was developed by Clum, Broyles, Borden, and Watkins (1990). It measures fearful cognitions that the person experienced during or after their last panic attack. It has shown to have good reliability and validity.

3. The Self-Efficacy Scales for Agoraphobia (SESA) was developed by S. Lloyd Williams at Stanford University (Williams 1982; Kinney and Williams 1988). This questionnaire asks the person to judge his or her ability to engage in various activities. The person rates his or her confidence in performing a graded sequence of feared tasks, on a scale from 0 to 100.

The client should fill out the PACQ and the SESA scales in the beginning, middle (after session 6), and at the end of treatment.

Specific Goals of Treatment and Limitations

Setting goals and striving to reach them gives you and your client direction and motivation. In the case of panic, the goal of most clients is for panics to cease. However, as much as they would never want to have another panic again, no treatment can guarantee it. Some clients hope to achieve this by taking medications. While medications can decrease their frequency and intensity, panic attacks are often not totally eliminated. In CBT, it is particularly useful to emphasize that the primary objective is to overcome the *fear of panic*. This is valid because once they overcome their fear, panic attacks usually stop or remain occasional occurrences. This reasoning also summarizes the essence of CBT and points to the work to be done by the client.

In agoraphobia, the client must formulate what he or she wants to accomplish. For instance, a person who has never driven on the freeway may not choose it as a goal. The therapist helps to modulate the goals in relationship to the number of sessions. Yet, particularly in agoraphobia work, progress often equals frequency and amount of *in vivo* exposure. Is the client willing to take risks, venturing to approach feared situations? How much time is he or she willing to devote to the assignments? Many clients will not have overcome all their avoidances during the course of this brief treatment. Hence, the importance of stating goals that *can* be reached is paramount.

In the mental health field there is increased attention being paid to the readiness state of the client, and the expectations the client has regarding the therapist's level of activity and support. The readiness state is much more explicitly addressed in the treatment of chemical dependence. These clients are very aware that they need to do hard work to overcome their addiction. They know that no pill or quick fix will accomplish it. When they consult a therapist, they are not always ready for that commitment. Some clients wish information first, and they need more time before they are ready. This is why comprehensive chemical dependency programs include educational groups for information, and decision groups where members explore what stands in the way of their making the commitment.

In contrast, many other mental health clients consult a therapist with the expectation that the therapist will fix his or her problem. Because of this, it can be very unclear in the initial interview how ready the client is to make the commitment to initiate demanding panic/phobia work. Therefore, it behooves you, the therapist, to ask the client at the end of the assessment session some questions to help determine their state of readiness and refer them to outside psychoeducational anxiety classes, if they are not ready to undergo treatment. If there is a mismatch between the client's readiness state and the treatment, the client is likely to feel dissatisfied and drop out.

The Use of Agenda Setting

The protocol illustrated here for the treatment of panic disorder and agoraphobia should be the first line of intervention for most clients, since the treatment and outcome are based on solid research. It provides a *nomothetic* formulation, i.e., a disorder-specific formulation with a treatment protocol based on proven efficacy. This protocol provides guidance and structure for the sessions. Yet you as a therapist may feel compelled to follow an *ideographic* formulation, i.e., one based on the client's ideosyncratic psychological mechanism rather than following a specific protocol. (See Jackeline Persons' book *Cognitive Therapy in Practice: A Case Formulation Approach*, 1989.) How do you strike a balance?

When offering treatment to the client, you must explore its length and cost. Who pays for the sessions? Is there a certain number of sessions provided? HMOs and managed care companies often set limits. Aside from these issues, what is the clients motivation? If considering brief treatment, it behooves you as the treating clinician to explain why a planned protocol must be followed. (Keep in mind that to closely follow a protocol is a greater challenge in individual than group therapy.) Yet flexibility depends in part on how closely the client does his or her homework assignments and stays focused on the work that must be accomplished. Finally, the cognitive restructuring, especially when working on core beliefs, is rather individualized, which takes you into an ideographic formulation.

Many prominent cognitive-behavior therapists have found that it works best to start each session with a review of the homework and setting an agenda. You will share which panic/phobia-specific work needs to be covered in that particular session. The client may bring up other problems over and beyond the panic/phobia work. By setting this agenda early in the session, you teach the client to prioritize the work, to manage time, to be focused on problems, and to take a problem-solving approach.

Clients can be very convincing in their need to talk about other problems. As a therapist, you need to be very alert to this, because *it is in the very nature of panic and agoraphobia to avoid dealing with frightening symptoms and situations.* Hence, the temptation to talk about other problems rather than take action to confront fears is great. It has been shown that clients benefit most from this treatment if they do not veer off course (Barlow, Presentation at Northern California Kaiser, October 1998). This means that you need to rather quickly, albeit gently, bring your client back to the agenda when he or she brings up other life issues.

The sessions are packed with a great deal of information and work to cover. Whenever a client brings up issues that take you to a different path, you may need to remind your client of possible session limits and that more sessions may be needed to finish the panic/phobia protocol. Someone will have to pay for the added sessions, either the managed care company or the client. One caveat is that, if safety questions arise (e.g., suicidal ideation), naturally they must be addressed first.

Homework

Homework is crucial because most changes occur outside the therapy sessions. It is an integral part of panic disorder to feel safer in company, especially in the company of a trusted therapist. But what does your client do when alone? He or she must learn to face and overcome fears alone in their territory.

The homework consists of reading the client manual, working with the worksheets, and doing interoceptive and *in vivo* exposures. Progress is measured via the self-rating scales. An excellent way to present the role of the homework initially is to say to your client that the therapy you do involves definite weekly home assignments. When you evaluate your client's readiness state, you may wish to tell your client that only they can overcome the panic/phobia symptoms, and you are there to guide the work. Your client must decide if he or she is ready to devote the necessary time and effort for a successful outcome.

Reviewing the homework in the *beginning* of each session allows both the client and therapist to establish the importance of homework and also helps with compliance. Exposures are recorded on worksheets provided for the client, indicating step, frequency, duration, etc. Self-reward is an integral part of goal-setting in agoraphobia. Unless this is addressed, clients often minimize their efforts. If the client has not done the homework, stumbling blocks, motivation, etc., can be reviewed.

Your client may not easily see the value of homework, may have too limited time available outside the sessions, may be too distressed by other problems, and may not feel ready for extensive work due to fear or comfort. In an open dialogue, you can help correct misconceptions and educate your client. When poor motivation for exposures is the problem, you can point out how much time avoidance often takes. In the case of fear, exposures can be planned in smaller, more manageable steps. Finally, your client needs to know that this disorder seldom remits on its own, especially the agoraphobic component.

Concurrent Pharmacological Treatment

Many panickers also take medications. There are pros and cons to combining the two treatments. The results of an excellent NIMH-sponsored, multi-site study on the efficacy of panic disorder (with not more than mild to moderate agoraphobia) showed at follow-up that clients did better *without* the concurrent use of antidepressants (Woods, Barlow, Gorman, et al. 1998). Benzodiazepines pose problems as well (Başoğlu 1992; Otto 1997). The advantages to CBT without concurrent medication treatment seem to be that this allows clients to trust themselves for the changes achieved, i.e., they attribute changes to their own efforts, and maybe they try harder in their cognitive-behavioral work. The result is increased confidence, especially if some improvement in symptoms occurs rapidly.

Clients who are not functioning well should be considered for medications. That is, if the client is missing work days, is extremely limited in his or her everyday life, or wishes to go on disability. It is almost always better for a client to function with medications than not to function. I am in principle opposed to disability because this feeds easily into agoraphobia. Also, when there are comorbidities (e.g., depression), medications *can* be considered. Regardless of the extent of the disorder, if a client is a strong believer in drug therapy and requests it, it should be offered as an option.

The two classes of medications approved by the NIH for panic disorder are antidepressants and high-potency benzodiazepines. While a number of tricyclic antidepressants (TCAs), such as imipramine, had proven very successful, the selective serotonin reuptake inhibitors (SSRIs) have greatly surpassed the TCAs in popularity. The SSRIs are easier tolerated. Paroxetine (Paxil) has been approved by the FDA for the treatment of panic disorder, and other SSRIs are awaiting approval. Monoamine oxidase inhibitors can be very powerful in the treatment, but because of their dietary restrictions and side-effect profile, they are used as a last resort.

The tranquilizers approved to date by the FDA for the treatment of panic disorder are alprazolam (Xanax) and clonazepam (Klonopin). These have shown positive results in double-blind, placebo-controlled studies. Lorazepam (Ativan) is also often used. Tranquilizers pose concern with physical and psychological dependence. Many psychiatrists therefore prescribe the tranquilizers more often initially, if at all, until the antidepressant takes effect. However, some clients take tranquilizers for prolonged periods, particularly if they cannot tolerate antidepressants. In that case clonazepam, with its longer half-life, is the better choice.

The quick effect of tranquilizers make them very attractive to many panickers, often taking them as soon as he or she feels any uncomfortable level of anxiety or has a panic attack. This can create strong psychological dependence. Hence, from a strictly psychological point, tranquilizers should be taken according to a schedule, not as needed. The problem that arises then is the increased risk of physical dependence.

Common Problems

Homework assignments, especially *in vivo* exposures, can pose great stumbling blocks. Clients find it very difficult to approach feared places and to engage in activities that provoke terror. While this is understandable, phobias will not subside without repeated exposures. Few clients approach exposures systematically enough to evoke minimum fear. Nonetheless, some steps can be taken to increase the probability of follow-through. First and foremost, your client's continued commitment depends on how well you track the assignments agreed upon. Second, behavioral aids in tracking are very helpful, which is why forms are provided to write down the assignments and report back from. Third, a careful plan helps, e.g., doing exposures with a coach first, repeating small exposures several times in a row (repeating "loops"), doing them often, and building rewards into the exposure plan. Group therapy lends itself particularly well to the follow-through with *in vivo* assignments, because the client sees how others struggle and accomplish their goals.

The best way to achieve compliance with reading assignments is to ask the client to report back on material read. I ask clients not to parrot back what I have said or what they have read, but rather what they found especially helpful, what they could relate to, points of controversy, etc. It should take only two to three minutes to make such a report.

Dealing with Managed Care Companies

If a managed-care company covers outpatient services, it is likely to pay for treatment of panic disorder. It will be to your advantage to inquire at the outset as to any limitations posed on such treatment and when and what kind of progress report you are expected to submit on behalf of your client. You will need to have your client sign a release of information, but give the minimum amount of information needed to the company. Document your treatment well. Keep your client informed of the limits and requirements. If further sessions are needed than were initially provided, request for them, citing literature that states that fifteen sessions is a common length of CBT treatment for this disorder (Gould, Otto, and Pollack 1995). If your request is denied and your client agrees to it, appeal the decision. A second denial may be difficult to overturn. Your client must decide with you the pros and cons of pursuing a second level of appeal. Because it is likely to be more time consuming, the cost of your time becomes an issue as well.

As targeted cognitive-behavior group therapy becomes more acceptable, managed care companies will understand that it is more cost-effective than individual therapy. One major stumbling block to group therapy for managed care is the logistic of keeping track of relevant groups for potential clients.

Termination and Follow-up

Relapse-prevention strategies constitute a definite component of treatment. What can the client expect? How can panic and phobias return? What increases the likelihood of fear returning? What are red flags to watch out for? How can the client be prepared? These questions are dealt with more explicitly in the last sessions.

This is also where the justification for assertiveness work and learning strategies to deal with worry patterns come in. The more the client learns to pay attention to and accept his or her own thoughts and feelings, the less such feelings get converted to anxiety. Likewise, the more a client is willing to take the risk of speaking up and setting limits with others, the more control he or she exercises. Assertiveness leads to a sense of control and mastery, and mastery is, in essence, incompatible with fear.

Appropriate termination is crucial in any therapy, including CBT. It is very helpful to plan booster sessions as a transition. If they are not planned, the client needs to know nonetheless that he or she can return if needed, and that a serious relapse is not a requirement for return. A temporary setback can be a good opportunity to go through a brief refresher.

The Assessment Session

Building an Initial Alliance

The goal of the initial encounter is to assess the problem as well as provide the client with a supportive, empathetic atmosphere where he or she feels safe. Although your technical skills and command of the treatment are important, the relationship is as crucial. The potential client needs to feel understood and respected. If the person leaves the session feeling that you are truly interested in helping him or her, the interviewee will likely become your client.

A good way to start the first encounter is by asking the person what brings them there. Clients usually have much they want to tell you, but they often report it in very unstructured ways. Hence, I find it best to ask the person to state *very briefly* what brings him or her to therapy. If the client states anything related to panic attacks, anxiety attacks, and/or any phobias, then I quickly move to a more structured way of interviewing. The reason is that you need answers to very specific questions to assess the diagnosis, and often a general way of reporting will not give you the answers in one session.

This session, as the remaining ones, must of necessity be very focused. Nonetheless, you can be very attentive, let your client elaborate a little, and make comments that show that you know what he or she is saying. Try to set up a full sixty minutes for this session.

Assessment

You need to conduct a good assessment in order to know where you will go with the treatment. This does not mean that you will not make mistakes or that other problems will not unfold as the work progresses. If you are going to apply disorder-targeted treatment in brief therapy, you cannot afford to flounder without direction. Major areas of assessment are outlined below, but this is not the order in which the questions are asked during the interview. At the end of this section are the types of questions needed for the diagnosis of panic disorder and agoraphobia. For a full assessment questionnaire, which covers all the areas stated herein, you may wish to consult *Treating Panic Disorder and Agoraphobia: A Step-by-Step Clinical Guide* (Zuercher-White 1997).

Potential clients have usually already told you or an intake worker over the telephone what the general problem is. Now you may wish to ask the person again to very briefly state what the nature of the problem is. Next, move quickly to specific questions that will ascertain the diagnosis of panic disorder. This will be followed by questions that also target the other areas described below.

Major Areas to Be Covered in the Assessment

1. **Urgent Conditions**

   Safety issues pertaining to suicidal or homicidal ideation are paramount. While it may be rare to encounter a panicker who is suicidal, it can occur. This is more likely if the person is also severely depressed. However, if you learn of a client's suicidal thoughts during the initial interview in response to your inquiry, then this is the first issue to be addressed. Is there a plan and an intent? Have there been attempts in the past? If you judge that hospitalization is not imminently needed, can your client give a "no-suicide" contract? This is best done in writing. Finally, I have found it very helpful to ask the person, "Can your word be trusted?" Most clients you meet are probably eager to be perceived as truthful and trustworthy, which gives some added weight to the contract.

2. **Medical Conditions**

   When did your interviewee have a medical check-up? If the panics started recently, has there been one since then? Does the client have medical conditions and take medications? It can be very helpful to get a signed release to speak to his or her physician. As you become more familiar with the disorder, you will be able to distinguish unusual symptoms or other uncommon occurrences. For instance, an elderly woman was referred by her physician to me for possible panic disorder. As I explored the manifestation of her condition, she reported that she would wake up at night drenched in sweat but essentially without fear. I shared my doubts about an anxiety disorder with her physician and she underwent further testing. It was eventually discovered that she suffered from sleep apnea. If the onset of panics is after age forty, if panic attacks have a temporal relationship with meals, if the symptom profile is different from that of typical panics, it is even more advisable to have a medical check-up.

3. **Medication Use**

   Does the client take prescribed or over-the-counter medicines? Some of them exacerbate anxiety, e.g., prednisone. Is he or she taking medications for this or another mental health condition?

4. Chemical Dependence (Substance Abuse)

The best way to approach this topic is to ask what quantities of alcohol or drugs the person consumes. Your assumption that some substance is ingested often decreases the likelihood of denial. Most of my clients simply say, "I don't take illegal drugs. I drink _____." General responses are best followed up with questions as to frequency per week or month and amount on any given day. As stated in the introduction, if a problem is detected, this needs to be addressed before panic treatment begins. Does the client ingest an excessive amount of caffeine, exacerbating his or her anxiety?

5. Determining the Presence of Panic Disorder and Agoraphobia

Keeping the *DSM-IV* diagnostic criteria in mind, determine the presence of panic attacks (Do they come on suddenly? What symptoms and how many are present?), panic disorder (Do panics occur unexpectedly? Has the client had at least two? Are there behavioral repercussions?), and agoraphobia (Is there avoidance of situations because of fear or does the client do them with extreme discomfort? If there is no current avoidance, was there in the past?). You need to briefly cover the course of the disorder (When did the panics first start? What precipitated the first panic? How frequent were the panics at their worst?) You also need to distinguish it from the *DSM-IV* condition agoraphobia without history of panic disorder. Is there or has there been significant functional impairment?

6. Assessing Comorbidities

You want to differentiate agoraphobia from other phobias, i.e., specific and social phobias. They often overlap. Fears can be diagnosed as specific phobias, social phobia, or agoraphobia. The differential diagnosis is based on the context in which the fears occur, history, severity, etc. (See *DSM-IV* also for other diagnoses mentioned in this chapter.)

To differentiate panic disorder from *generalized anxiety disorder* (GAD), ask about worry patterns (excessive worry, worries about very small things), and symptoms (tenseness, irritability, difficulty concentrating, restlessness, etc.). Is this a major problem, and if so, since when? If the client states that the worry started after the first panic attack, it is most likely part of the panic disorder syndrome. If it's very extreme, and/or it preceded the panic, a GAD diagnosis might be appropriate. To assess the presence of *obsessive-compulsive disorder*, ask the interviewee if he or she has intrusive thoughts or compulsive rituals. To assess depression, you may ask for general mood level, interest in usual activities, withdrawal from others, feelings of guilt and failure, thoughts and plans of suicide.

By the time you finish the assessment, you may have detected a possible personality disorder, but this may not become evident until you work with the client. If it emerges, does it interfere with treatment? Are modifications needed?

7. Past Treatment and Family History

Has the client received treatment for panic disorder or for another condition in the past? You may wish to inquire whether the client found the treatment helpful. Is there a family history of emotional problems and mental illness, including treatments?

8. **Job/Family Situation**

   Ask about work and family, including if there are tensions in these settings. Is the family life positive? Does the client feel satisfied with work?

9. **The Mental Status Exam: Current Level of Functioning**

   The areas to be covered are:

   a) *Appearance:* grooming and outward signs of health

   b) *Behavior:* verbal and nonverbal, and interactional style

   c) *Mood and affect* (range of emotions): symptoms of depression and anxiety, excessive anger; sleep, appetite, energy level

   d) *Accuracy of perception:* illusions, hallucinations

   e) *Sensorium:* level of consciousness, orientation, concentration

   f) *Memory:* past and recent

   g) *Intelligence:* portrayed by educational/occupational status, vocabulary, etc.

   h) *Insight and judgment:* insight into the problems; use of common sense and problem-solving ability

   i) *Thought content and process:* obsessions, morbid preoccupation, loosening of associations, etc.

   j) *Suicidal/homicidal ideation:* current and past, ideation versus plan, indications *against* carrying out a plan

10. **Strengths, Coping Skills, Resources, and Support System**

    What is the client bringing into the treatment as far as strengths to balance against the problems? For instance, the client may perceive himself or herself as a strong person, as being very sensitive, as being the one whom others have leaned on. In these cases, try to find ways in the treatment to mobilize these strengths.

    How has the client attempted to cope with this condition or with other difficult situations in the past? Can any of these skills be utilized now? For instance, has the client resorted to very helpful self-talk? Is he or she assertive? Does the client exercise regularly? Does the client have a support system? Can he or she talk to someone trusted? Is he or she involved in a support group?

Some Assessment Questions

- *Have you ever had an episode of sudden, intense anxiety?*

- *How long does it take for the symptoms to rise to a peak?*

- *What symptoms have you had with these sudden anxiety episodes?*

- *In what situations have you had these intense panic attacks?*

- *Have they ever come totally out of the blue?*

- *Do you fear the panic attacks themselves or what they may lead to?*

- *Do you use certain objects (medications, water, etc.) or engage in certain behaviors (sit down, look for an exit, etc.) to feel safe from panics?*

- *Have you had a medical-workup since the panic attacks started?*

- *Do you have a medical illness explaining the symptoms?*

- *Does fear prevent you from doing certain things or going to a number of places that are not avoided by most people?*

- *Is the fear of panics or panic-like symptoms what mainly keeps you from doing the things you described?*

- *Has the fear of panics interfered with your work, traveling, or doing other things you like to do?*

Sharing Your Conclusions Regarding Diagnosis

Once you have established the diagnosis, share your conclusion and diagnosis.

Panic Disorder Without Agoraphobia

"It appears that you suffer from panic disorder. This is a very treatable condition. You are fortunate that you have not developed agoraphobia as well. I also urge you strongly not to start to avoid situations because of fear of panics. Although it may feel good to do so at the moment, you make your condition worse if you start dealing with anxiety by avoiding. You could end up with two conditions instead of only one. Panic disorder by itself is bad enough, agoraphobia on top of it makes it much worse. See, avoidance does not make panic disorder go away. It makes it much worse as time goes on."

Panic Disorder with Minimal, Very Recent Avoidance

"You are indeed suffering from panic disorder. It is very understandable that once you have panic attacks, you want to avoid certain situations for fear of these panics. It feels good at the moment to escape or avoid. However, each time you give in to fear that way, you will lose a little more of your self-confidence. Avoidance does not make panic disorder go away. Rather, you can end up with two conditions instead of just panic disorder, which in itself is bad enough. You can develop what is called agoraphobia as well. While also treatable, this is a much more difficult condition. I would very strongly urge you to try not to avoid anything but to continue leading a normal life, with or without panics. If you end up escaping from a situation because of anxiety and panic, try to go back to the situation *as soon as possible*.

Panic Disorder with Agoraphobia

"You are suffering from panic disorder and agoraphobia. Agoraphobia is the term used when you avoid a number of situations for fear of having panic attacks. This is a treatable condition, though it requires a lot of work.

Client Goals

Working with goals is crucial in short-term therapy. You model the importance by asking your client in a general way what he or she hopes to achieve with therapy. You can also start to teach your client the importance of behaviorally stated goals by asking for them. For instance, "I want to feel better," can be followed up with, "What would be different, and what would you do differently if you felt better?" If your client says "I want to be rid of panics," or "I don't want to feel anxiety," you may be able to gently state that no treatment can guarantee absence of panics, and that getting rid of anxiety while they are alive is not possible. Then you can rephrase these statements by stating goals that are likely to be reached. For instance, "Of course, the ideal is never to have panics again. But if you had an occasional panic, and had *no fear*, would you think it would be a worthwhile goal? Think of bad headaches. They cannot be totally eliminated; they happen, but most people don't fear them." As stated in the introduction, goals in phobias must closely be linked to the time and effort the client is willing to devote.

Treatment Recommendations

Cognitive-Behavior Therapy

"The psychological treatment of choice for panic disorder is cognitive-behavior therapy. 'Cognitive' pertains to thoughts, and 'behavior' naturally to behaviors, i.e., actions. This treatment has been well researched and produces very good results. But it requires work.

"The treatment consists of the following parts:

1. *Psychoeducation.* In this section you will learn about anxiety, how panic attacks are produced physiologically, and how to recognize the different components of the panic response.

2. *Diaphragmatic breathing.* Many panic attacks are associated with hyperventilation. About a third of panickers (i.e., people with panic disorder) hyperventilate chronically, but most of them do not know they are doing it. You will learn diaphragmatic breathing as a way to stop hyperventilation. It will also help slow down other physical symptoms in panic or high anxiety. Many people find it a very useful coping skill.

3. *Changing fearful thoughts.* People with panic and phobias have fears such as the one(s) you mentioned (heart attack, fainting, strokes, losing control, etc.). These are generally called 'catastrophic thoughts.' As long as you be-

lieve that panic attacks are dangerous over and above the intense discomfort they produce, you keep scaring yourself. And we know that *fear is the ingredient that mostly feeds the panic cycle.* Therefore, there is a great deal of work that goes into changing the catastrophic thoughts and hopefully overcoming the fear.

4. *Interoceptive exercises.* 'Interoceptive' is a technical term meaning feedback from within the body. Fear also seems to become conditioned, so we work on this fear behaviorally as well. These are little exercises that you can do that bring on symptoms similar to those in panic, which are then repeated until you no longer fear them. The idea is that when you have a panic again, you will no longer be afraid of these sensations.

5. (If agoraphobia is present) *In vivo exposure.* Phobic fears are overcome by exposure to the feared situation. Exposure brings about confidence in your ability to deal with the anxiety elicited. You may have tried to do exposures in the past without much success. You will learn how to plan exposures so that they have the intended result: a decrease of fear.

6. *Adjuncts to Success and Relapse Prevention.* We will also work on strategies to deal with chronic worry, assertiveness, and relapse prevention."

Pharmacotherapy

"Let's briefly go over the issue of medications, since you are likely to have thought about them. There are pros and cons. Two main types of medications are used in panic disorder: antidepressants and tranquilizers. Antidepressants help greatly with anxiety. They have to be taken daily but do not produce dependence. The down side is that they often have side effects, though these vary from person to person. Antidepressants have to be taken usually for at least a few months. Though it's sometimes also hard to get off antidepressants (because of return of symptoms), this is more pronounced with tranquilizers.

"Tranquilizers, while tolerated more easily, can produce physical and/or psychological dependence. When taken daily for a number of weeks or months, they are likely to produce physical dependence. This means that they have to be tapered off slowly, and it is often hard to get off them. On the other hand, if taken as needed when feeling high anxiety or panic, they are likely to produce psychological dependence."

If the client is not already taking medications, you may want to recommend when to consider them, in some instances. Also, a client taking medications may wish to hear your opinion. Some guidelines follow.

New Panicker (No or Mild Phobias)

"Since you are a panicker with a rather short history and have no agoraphobia (or: your condition is on the mild side, and/or your agoraphobia is mild), you may wish to do the treatment without medications. As I described above, there are advantages. As you improve, you will have full confidence that those improvements are a result of your efforts and learning. If you can tolerate the symptoms for a while and want to rely on your own resources, you may want to hold off with medications for now. If you decide not to take medications now but later feel that you have not improved enough or have a much harder time than you expected, then you can always consult a psychiatrist for medications at that time. What do you think?"

Client with Severe Panics and Significant Agoraphobia

"If you feel that you are having a very hard time and for whatever reason cannot tolerate the symptoms, you may choose to take medications as well. They will help you feel better faster than the cognitive-behavioral learning alone. Remember that phobias do not go away with medications. You want to still learn the skills so that you can eventually get off medications. If you do not get off them before we finish the treatment, and if you find yourself having a hard time when you taper, you may choose to come for a brief refresher course. If you choose not to take medications now, we will keep close track on how you are progressing and medications can be introduced at a later time, if needed."

There Is Significant Functional Impairment and/or Serious Comorbidity

(The person is not working, is becoming housebound, is depressed with vegetative signs, is suicidal, etc.) "You are having a very difficult time, and because of this I recommend that you consider medications. It is definitely better to function with medications than not function at all. It is extremely important that you work and do some other basic things; otherwise you might become more limited, even end up housebound. This would be infinitely worse than having to take medications. Also, being very depressed or extremely anxious, you may have a hard time attending to the task at hand. Remember that the cognitive-behavioral treatment is hard work."

Homework: For a Successful Outcome

(This section is inspired by the approach of Dr. David Burns, as shared by him at a Presentation at Kaiser, July 1998. Dr. Burns' research has shown that compliance with homework assignments in cognitive therapy is extremely crucial to overcome the disorders.)

"As you gather from the explanation I gave about the treatment, it requires your active collaboration. It may be very different from traditional psychotherapy you may have gone through before or heard of. This treatment does not work by just coming to and learning in the sessions. For you to really overcome your anxiety problem, you need to work very hard in between sessions. You need to put into practice the new skills you will be learning. Monitoring progress is crucial. And finally, *my* agenda is for you not only to overcome your problem now, but be better able to deal with these types of problems in the future—essentially for you to become your own therapist.

"To be more specific about homework, I will ask you to monitor the number and severity of panics. I will ask you to fill out self-rating scales on fear of panic sensations, and (if agoraphobia is present) your confidence in doing various activities. Throughout treatment, there will be reading assignments and worksheets to work with from the *client manual*. If you have *no agoraphobic avoidance,* you need to plan on about two hours of homework a week."

If agoraphobia is present: "A significant part of your therapy includes doing exposures to fearful situations. You need to set aside time to do exposures *at least* three times a week, and *at least* six hours per week in total. The more often you do the exposures, and the more time you devote to them, the faster and better you will progress. People do best who attend the sessions regularly and do their agreed-upon assignments."

"If you decide to embark on this treatment, the contract that I will ask you to sign includes your agreement to the homework. Do you feel that you are ready to do this treatment, including setting aside time for the homework I described?" (If the client says "Yes," answer, "At the end of this session I will ask you to start with some homework.")

If the client is hesitant in regards to the last question, you may wish to explore the reasons. As Dr. Burns suggests, take an active role in soliciting possible reasons. These could be: dependency issues, helplessness, believing in a medical model, holding a traditional view of therapy, thinking that it should be done when he or she feels like doing it, etc. Yet whatever the reason, if your client cannot devote the time needed, he or she should wait for a later time when ready. Otherwise the client is likely to drop out and may lose faith in this mode of therapy.

Length of Treatment and Specific Goals

The treatment is roughly divided into four modules. In panic disorder without agoraphobia, each module consists of three sessions; in panic disorder with agoraphobia, you may need from two to four additional sessions, depending on the extent of avoidance and how diligently the client has been working on his or her phobias, i.e., the time spent on exposures. However, as mentioned earlier, more sessions may be needed with some clients, especially when comorbid conditions are present. Hence, length of treatment depends on the presence of agoraphobia and overall severity. Encourage your client to set goals that he or she thinks can be achieved within a brief therapy modality. At the end of the assessment session you can ask your client to set up one specific phobia-related goal, which will become part of the homework.

Panic Disorder Without Agoraphobia

"You can expect treatment to take twelve weeks, with one therapy session a week. This will depend on whether we stay close to the steps we need to cover for a successful treatment. The more you are willing to follow through with the assignments in between sessions, the faster we will progress. If other issues are extensive enough that we do not achieve our session-by-session panic agenda, the panic treatment will take that much longer. If you like, when you bring up other issues, I will let you know if they sidetrack our panic work, and together we may want to decide how to proceed."

Panic Disorder with Agoraphobia

"You can expect treatment to take sixteen weeks, with one therapy session a week. We will need to be rather task-oriented in order to achieve good results. The more you are willing to follow through with the assignments in between sessions, the faster we will progress. If you bring up other issues, we will need to determine where to put our efforts. This is because if other issues are extensive enough that we do not achieve our session-by-session panic/phobia agenda, treatment will take that much longer."

If agoraphobia is present: A part of each session will be devoted to agoraphobic assignments, i.e., following up on exposures done since the last session, and planning new ones. Because of this, you might plan on spreading out the panic work. Think of the panic treatment as consisting of four modules: Module I: psychoeducation and breathing retraining (treatment sessions 1–3); Module II: cognitive restructuring (treatment sessions 4–6); Module III: interoceptive exposure (treatment sessions 7–9); Module IV: strategies to deal with chronic worry and nonassertiveness and relapse prevention (sessions 10–12). In agoraphobia, consider spreading out the work in one of these ways (options a and b might be better than c):

(a) Space out each module to four sessions, e.g., Module I: treatment sessions 1 through 4, and so forth.

(b) Keep the work of each module to three sessions, and add one session after each module to concentrate more on agoraphobia work. The added sessions can also be used for therapist-aided exposures.

(c) Do most of the work as suggested over the twelve sessions (as with panic-only work), and add four sessions at the very end exclusively for agoraphobia work.

Summary of Session

"We have finished with the evaluation. I have recommended cognitive-behavior therapy, which I briefly broke down into the main components. We have reviewed medications and agreed that you will/will not start with drug treatment at this time. We also reviewed the expected length of treatment and the work that is involved for you."

Consent to Treatment and Feedback from Client

Have a generic Consent to Treatment form (see suggested format) for panic and phobias prepared in advance. The consent form should include the following information: the nature of the treatment you plan to provide, expected benefits and potential risks (e.g., the risk involves anxiety, even high levels, when encountering phobic exposures), alternative treatments and their efficacy, limits to confidentiality (based on your state laws), and a delineation of fees and payment schedule (including late cancels and no shows). Have the client read and sign the consent form in the session, or take it home and and bring it back to the first treatment session. (Have extras in case your client forgets it and/or your client wants a copy.) If a third party payor is involved, get a release of information signed.

"Do you have any questions or concerns? Was there anything I said that was not clear to you or that made you feel uncomfortable? In order for us to work together, we must feel comfortable and understand each other."

Homework

"Now that you have agreed to treatment, I will ask you to do a few homework assignments for our next session. You can also find them in your client manual."

1. I would like you to read and be ready to sign this treatment contract. It states some basic points about the treatment on which you are embarking. It also states that for this treatment to be successful, you need to spend some time doing homework assignments. If you have any questions before our next treatment session, call me. Otherwise I will have you sign a copy of this contract in the beginning of our next session.

2. Fill out Worksheet 1: Panic Frequency and Intensity, the PACQ, and (if agoraphobia is present) the SESA. These scales and worksheet allow us to assess how you are progressing with overcoming your panic and phobia symptoms over time. If you have not done it, I will ask you to fill them out in the beginning of the next session, but it will significantly cut into our work and put us behind.

3. Read the introduction and assessment chapters in the client manual. Please comment on points that stood out and bring up questions.

If agoraphobia is present:

4. Fill out one goal on Worksheet 9: Goal and the Steps to Achieve It. We do not have time to review this worksheet today, but the example that follows (on page 123 in your client manual) will give you an idea. Please set up *one* goal for the next session. Ideally, think of a goal that is particularly relevant for you and that can be broken down into steps, for instance, goals related to driving or going to stores and malls. We will look at it next time and prepare you for setting up other goals.

Please Note: You will find Worksheets 9 (page 156) and 10 (page 159), and Therapist Records 9T (page 158) and 10T (page 160) in the Chapter titled "Sessions 1–16."

Schedule the next appointment.

Consent to Treatment

I, _____, agree to provide cognitive-behavior therapy to _____ for the condition of _____. This modality has been shown empirically to be the suitable therapy for panic and phobias. It involves a great deal of homework, which consists of reading, worksheets, and exposure therapy. If you have agoraphobia, you need to do at least six hours of exposure to feared situations weekly. Without doing the homework we agree on, you are not likely to benefit much from the treatment. The risk of this treatment involves temporary feelings of anxiety when confronting feared situations. The expected benefits are that you will be able to overcome your fears.

While some clients with these types of fears have been treated with other psychotherapeutic modalities, the latter have not shown the same efficacy as cognitive-behavior therapy. Medications can help with panic and phobias while the person takes them but often do not have a lasting positive effect after stopping them. This is because medications do not teach you skills or engender confidence in the person. However, some people feel they need to take medications also.

Our sessions are confidential, with some specific limitations posed by law, such as my duty to take action or inform if you are in danger to harm yourself or others intentionally as a result of an emotional disorder.

My fee is _____ an hour. If you cancel later than _____, you will be charged full fee.

Your signature affirms that you understand and agree with these points. This includes the homework involved. These points can be discussed and clarified at any time.

_____   _____

(Therapist)   (Client)

_____

Date of signatures

Worksheet 1:
Panic Frequency and Intensity

Name: _____   Month & Year: _____

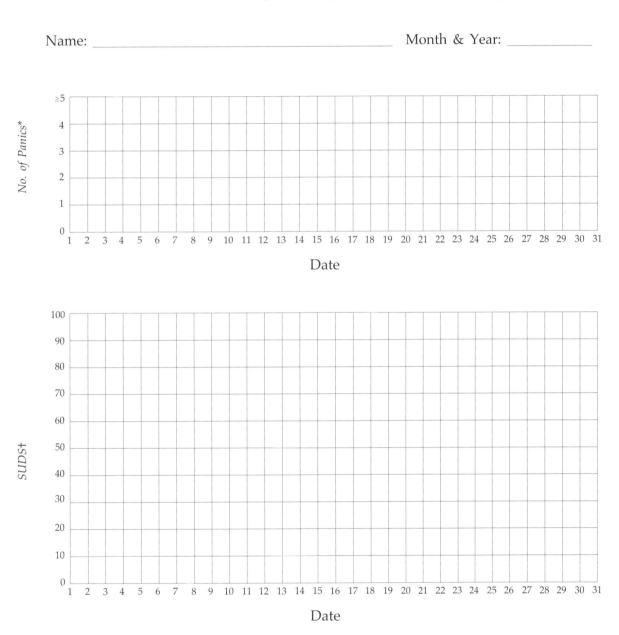

---

* Panic is defined here as a very sudden, intense surge of fear.

† If one or more panics, rate highest SUDS. SUDS: Subjective Units of Anxiety-Distress Scale.
  0 = Totally calm, no anxiety or fear. 50 = Moderate level of anxiety/fear. 100 = Intolerable level of anxiety/fear.

Panic Attack Cognitions Questionnaire (PACQ) *

Frightening thoughts often accompany or follow panic attacks. If you were to have a panic attack right now, use the scale below to rate each of the following thoughts according to the degree to which you would think it to be true.

1 = Not at all
2 = Some, but not much
3 = Quite a lot
4 = Would totally dominate my thoughts

1. I am going to die. _____

2. I am going insane. _____

3. I am losing control. _____

4. This will never end. _____

5. I am really scared. _____

6. I am having a heart attack. _____

7. I am going to pass out. _____

8. I don't know what people will think. _____

9. I won't be able to get out of here. _____

10. I don't understand what is happening to me. _____

11. People will think I am crazy. _____

12. I will always be this way. _____

13. I am going to throw up. _____

14. I must have a brain tumor. _____

15. I am going to act foolish. _____

16. I am going blind. _____

17. I will hurt someone. _____

18. I am going to have a stroke. _____

19. I am going to scream. _____

20. I will be paralyzed by fear. _____

21. Something is really physically wrong with me. _____

22. I will not be able to breathe. _____

23. Something terrible will happen. _____

---

* Used with permission of the authors, Clum, Broyles, Borden, and Watkins (1990).

Self-Efficacy Scales for Agoraphobia (SESA)[*]

Instructions

The following questionnaire asks about your confidence in your ability to do various activities. Each activity consists of several tasks. Indicate next to each task how confident you are that you could do that task if you were to try it right now. Assume that a trusted companion drove you to and from each activity away from home.

There are two columns to rate your confidence:

- Under the first column, "Alone," rate your confidence while you attempt the tasks alone.

- Under the second column, "Accompanied by Friend," rate your confidence assuming that the companion goes with you while you attempt the tasks.

Rate your confidence in both columns for all tasks by entering a number from the scale below.

Confidence Scale

0	10	20	30	40	50	60	70	80	90	100
can not do	very uncertain				moderately certain					certain

Confidence (0–100)

	Alone	Accompanied by Friend
1. Driving an automobile. How confident are you that you could		
Drive 10 blocks making turns in a quiet residential area, then return to start.	_____	_____
Drive 10 blocks on a minor thoroughfare with a few traffic lights, then return to start (1 mile/1.6 km).	_____	_____
Drive 10 blocks on a major thoroughfare with many traffic lights, then return to start (1 mile/1.6 km).	_____	_____

---

[*] Used with permission of the authors, Williams (1982) and Kinney and Williams (1988).

Drive 1 exit (2 miles) on a busy freeway
(expressway) in the right hand lane, then return
to start.

Drive 5 exits (10 miles) on a busy freeway
(expressway), changing lanes, then return to
start.

2. Heights. Imagine a tall residential building that
has balconies on every floor with waist-high
railings. How confident are you that you could

Go to the 2nd floor (the first floor above ground
level) and look over the railing straight down at
the ground for 15 seconds.

Go to the 3rd floor and look over the railing
straight down at the ground for 15 seconds.

Go to the 4th floor and look over the railing
straight down at the ground for 15 seconds.

Go to the 6th floor and look over the railing
straight down at the ground for 15 seconds.

Go to the 10th floor and look over the railing
straight down at the ground for 15 seconds.

3. Walking away from your home.
How confident are you that you could

Walk away from your home for a distance of 1
block.

Walk away from your home for a distance of 3
blocks.

Walk away from your home for a distance of 5
blocks.

Walk away from your home for a distance of 7
blocks.

Walk away from your home for a distance of 10
blocks (1 mile / 1.6 km).

4. Flying in a jet airplane. How confident are you that you could

    Enter an airport terminal, go to a passenger boarding area, stay there 15 minutes, and leave without flying.   _____ _____

    Sit in an airplane, taxi around the runway for 15 minutes, and then return to the terminal and leave.   _____ _____

    Take a 20 minute flight.   _____ _____

    Take a 1 hour flight.   _____ _____

    Take a 5 hour flight   _____ _____

5. Going distances from home. How confident are you that you could go the following distances from home if you were to drive there, and remain there for 1 hour before returning.

    5 blocks.   _____ _____

    1 mile (1.6 km).   _____ _____

    5 miles (8 km).   _____ _____

    10 miles (16 km).   _____ _____

    50 miles (80 km).   _____ _____

6. Driving across bridges. How confident are you that you could

    Drive across a short freeway overpass (distance—1 city block).   _____ _____

    Drive across a long freeway overpass (distance—3 city blocks).   _____ _____

    Drive across a bridge over a river (distance—1/2 mile/.8 km).   _____ _____

    Drive across a 1 mile (1.6 km) long bridge close to the water.   _____ _____

Drive across a 2 mile (3.2 km) long bridge high
over the water.

_____   _____

7. Riding an elevator in a 10-story office building.
How confident are you that you could

Walk into the elevator, close the door part way,
then open it and walk out.

_____   _____

Ride the elevator up 1 floor, and return on it.

_____   _____

Ride the elevator up 3 floors, and return on it.

_____   _____

Ride the elevator up 6 floors, and return on it.

_____   _____

Ride the elevator up 10 floors, and return on it.

_____   _____

8. Sitting at the rear of a city bus.
How confident are you that you could

Ride 1 block in a fairly empty city bus.

_____   _____

Ride 1 block in a crowded city bus.

_____   _____

Ride 3 blocks in a crowded city bus.

_____   _____

Ride 10 blocks in a crowded city bus.

_____   _____

Ride 5 miles (8 km) in a crowded city bus.

_____   _____

9. Tolerating closed-in places. How confident are
you that you could go into a small room, 5 ft x 5 ft,
without lights or windows, close the door and then

Sit for 15 seconds.

_____   _____

Sit for 1 minute.

_____   _____

Sit for 3 minutes.

_____   _____

Sit for 5 minutes.

_____   _____

Sit for 20 minutes.

_____   _____

10. Imagine a crowded movie theater with 30 rows of seats and an aisle down the center. How confident are you that you could

Sit in the back row on the aisle for 5 minutes. _____ _____

Sit in the 10th row from the rear of the theater, 5 seats in from the aisle for 10 minutes. _____ _____

Sit halfway to the front of the theater, in the middle of the row, for 10 minutes. _____ _____

Sit 10 rows from the front of the theater, in the middle of the row, for 20 minutes. _____ _____

Sit 5 rows from the front of the theater, in the middle of the row, for an entire 1 1/2 hour film. _____ _____

11. Walking across a bridge. Think of a long automobile/pedestrian bridge that stands about 50 feet off the ground, is about 500 feet long, and whose middle passes over a river 100 feet wide. How confident are you that, starting at the beginning of the bridge, you could

Walk 100 feet across and return to the beginning. _____ _____

Walk 200 feet across and return to the beginning. _____ _____

Walk 300 feet across and return to the beginning. _____ _____

Walk 400 feet across and return to the beginning. _____ _____

Walk 500 feet across and return to the beginning. _____ _____

12. Shopping at a supermarket. How confident are you that you could

Without a shopping cart, walk once all the way around the inside of the store, to all four corners, and then exit. _____ _____

Select 4 items from various parts of the store
and wait in line 2 minutes before checking out.   _____   _____

Select 10 items from various parts of the store
and wait in line 5 minutes before checking out.   _____   _____

Order an item from the meat or deli counter
employee, select 10 other items, and wait inline   _____   _____
10 minutes before checking out.

Select 30 items from various parts of the store,
including items from the meat or deli counter   _____   _____
employee, and wait inline 15 minutes before
checking out.

13. Walking along a busy city street.
    How confident are you that you could

    Walk 1 block and return to the start.   _____   _____

    Walk 3 blocks and return to the start.   _____   _____

    Walk 5 blocks and return to the start.   _____   _____

    Walk 7 blocks and return to the start.   _____   _____

    Walk 10 blocks and return to the start.   _____   _____

14. Walking through an indoor shopping mall.
    Think of an average indoor shopping mall that
    runs in a straight line from a large department
    store at one end of the mall, to another department
    store at the other end of the mall, with many smaller
    shops lining the mall. The total distance from the
    outside of one department store to the outside of the
    other is about 750 feet. How confident are you that,
    starting at the outside of one department store, you could

    Walk through the first department store and a
    few steps into the mall, then return to where
    you started.   _____   _____

    Walk through the first department store and
    walk an additional 150 feet through the mall,
    then return to where you started.   _____   _____

Walk through the first department store and walk an additional 300 feet through the mall, then return to where you started.

        _____ _____

Walk through the first department store and walk an additional 450 feet to the entrance of the second department store, then return to where you started.

        _____ _____

Walk through the first department store and walk an additional 450 feet to the second department store, then walk through the second department store to the outside door, then return to where you started.

        _____ _____

15. Being in a restaurant that has both a counter and tables, how confident are you that you could

Stay for 1 minute at the counter.

        _____ _____

Order a beverage, stay 10 minutes at the counter.

        _____ _____

Order a meal while sitting at a table far from the exit then:

        _____ _____

Stay 10 minutes.

        _____ _____

Stay 20 minutes.

        _____ _____

Session 1

The Physiology of Fear and Panic Attacks

Monitoring of Current Status

Review with the client the two or three self-rating scales: Worksheet 1: Panic Frequency and Intensity, the PACQ and, if agoraphobia is present, the SESA. (Review them quickly—at this time you want simply the baseline.) This review becomes a good lead-in to inquire about general mood level. If depression was indicated during the assessment, you already know to follow up on this closely. Other times the client may reveal an unexpected deep depression. For instance, if scores are high (e.g., panic frequency), you may take the opportunity to inquire about depression, and if so, suicidal ideation. In these instances, you need to revisit the diagnostic question. There might be an added diagnosis of major depression, which may for a while become the focus of attention. If the scores are low, comment on the fact that the client seems to be feeling rather well.

Crisis/Safety Issues

If there is a safety-related issue such as suicidal or homicidal ideation or there is another major crisis, it must be dealt with first, taking precedence over anything else. Questions to ask are:

- What does the ideation consist of?

- Is there a plan for action? Is the client likely to follow through? Has there been similar acting-out behavior in the past?

- Does the client need hospitalization? Is there a need to report a threat of harm to someone else? Does a child or elder abuse report need to be made?

(You must know the reporting laws in the state you practice in and how the psychotherapist-patient privilege applies.)

- If there is no need for hospitalization, is the client able to make a no-suicide contract, preferably in writing?

If satisfied with the current risk assessment, tell your client that you will be checking up on this in upcoming sessions, all the while maintaining a positive expectation of improvement.

Review Medication Use

If your client is taking a medication, ask if he or she is taking it as prescribed and whether there are any major problems. A number of clients may need your encouragement in following through with it. If there are complaints of side effects, listen to what they are, and encourage your client to speak with the prescribing physician, who could end up changing the dose or prescribing another medication.

Sometimes issues regarding tranquilizer use come up. For instance, the client may say that he or she is taking tranquilizers three times a day and wishes to cut back. If you believe that this is a good idea, you could tell the client that you want to discuss it with the prescribing psychiatrist. Other times, the client may have tranquilizers prescribed by his or her regular physician, and he or she may tell you that the physician just gave the tranquilizer as a way to quickly deal with the problem. You may ask how often it says on the prescription to use it. It is preferable for you to be able to read the label on the medication itself. In this case, you may tell your client that you will confer with the physician (make sure you have a release of information signed, or if in house, at least a verbal agreement), and you or the physician will get back to him or her.

Update on Events/Concerns Since Last Session

Unless a major issue came up when reviewing the self-rating scales, ask the client if there is a significant event or important concern that occurred since the last session. You can add that this is so you know if something must be added to the agenda. If the client answers affirmatively, ask him or her to describe it *very briefly*. If your client elaborates too much, remind him or her that you need to know just enough to place the issue on the agenda. If the issue is not too pressing, tell the client that you will next proceed with the agenda for the day and leave about ten minutes at the end of the session to work on the new issue. It might be helpful here to say a word or two on how it will be addressed. For instance, you might state that the issue seems to require a problem-solving approach, or that the client may need to vent his or her feelings about the issue.

As I mentioned in the introduction, clients can find many ways to avoid dealing with their panic and phobias (one way to avoid is not to talk, think, or read about it). Hence, distinguish an occasional significant issue from the tendency to repeatedly talk about general experiences and feelings. The latter may take the place of doing the work required to overcome this disorder.

Agenda

Begin your planned agenda for this session by summarizing the interventions that you will be covering. This shows that you are following a planned treatment agenda and allows your client to orient him/herself to the task at hand.

In session 1, you will cover the physiology of fear and panic. This lays the groundwork for the skills you will subsequently teach your client. Precisely because the panic symptoms are not inherently dangerous, and there is an explanation for each symptom, the feared catastrophic outcomes are unfounded.

After the psychoeducational component, you will teach your client to recognize the various components of a panic attack. This helps your client to increasingly view the panic attack as a response, a process, rather than an entity that engulfs him or her and over which there is no control. Your client will learn more and more how to intervene in different places along the panic process.

Review of Homework

This is a good time to review the client's homework assignment. By giving homework already in the assessment session, and by reviewing the homework early in each session, you continually emphasize its importance.

Observe: For logistical purposes, the agoraphobia homework assignments are listed at the end of the homework list. In actuality, you may want to start the session monitoring the current status via Worksheet 1, followed by the agenda and, if agoraphobia is present, by a review of the agoraphobia assignments (what has been accomplished and planning new ones). Then you may turn to the rest of the homework, which leads well into the work that follows.

The homework assignments that you are following up since the assessment session are:

1. Reading the written treatment contract and preparing to sign it. After answering any questions raised, present them with a new copy to sign. (Your client can keep one copy.)

2. Completing the self-rating scales: Worksheet 1: Panic Frequency and Intensity, PACQ, and SESA. (These may have been reviewed in the very beginning of the session.)

3. Reading the introduction and assessment chapters in the client manual.

If agoraphobia is present:

4. Filling out one goal on Worksheet 9: Goal and the Steps to Achieve It.

If your client did not complete a homework assignment, explore any lack of clarity with the task, motivational issues, and/or resistance. It behooves you to do this at any time during treatment.

Concepts and Skills

Skill Building

Coping Behaviors and Statements

"As you work with me and your client manual, I want you to become a participant-observer. You will not just observe (by listening to me and reading the material), but you need to actively participate in your treatment. Please bring a therapy pad (a pad of paper you use only in therapy) and/or binder and a pen to all sessions, so that you can jot down anything you find particularly useful. Also think of things you can learn to do or say to yourself when encountering a panic or phobic situation.

"Intense fear has an impact on many people by rendering them emotionally paralyzed and mentally confused and unable to reason. They feel overwhelmed and stuck in the fear mode. This fear makes them feel out of control. Control can be reclaimed by mobilizing the mental, emotional, and behavioral coping skills.

"Once you identify these coping behaviors and statements, write them down on Worksheet 2: My Personal Coping Affirmations. Let us look at one example of a possible statement: "Don't bolt! I will stay put and continue doing what I was doing, even if it is hard." This means that as you progress in treatment, you will practice staying in the situation where you are having a panic or in a phobic situation rather than escape. Once you learn diaphragmatic breathing, you may want to put down "Do diaphragmatic breathing." A third example would be "When anxious, identify the fear and challenge it (with Worksheet 4).

"Instead of my giving you a list of affirmations, you will be creating your own with the statements and reminders that you find most helpful. See if you can capture something particularly helpful in each session and chapter. Please bring the coping affirmations worksheet with you at all times. I will be asking you off and on what you have on it, especially when you describe to me difficult panic and phobic situations you encounter. This way, when things get difficult for you, we will be able to refer back and remember what you've thought would be particularly helpful."

Psychoeducation

Self-Reward

"The work you have ahead of you is going to be hard. Use rewards to help you stay motivated. Rewards work best if you plan them *in advance* of difficult steps and goals. In agoraphobic situations, Worksheet 9 asks you to specifically set up a meaningful reward when you reach your goal. But you need to also reward yourself for steps in between. I cannot emphasize enough the value of rewarding yourself.

"Consider material rewards such as buying yourself something not too expensive, activities you like to do alone or with others. In either case, always try to reinforce your accomplishments by giving yourself a pat on the back, telling yourself that you have done well whenever you have completed an exposure or feel you've handled a panic attack well."

The Physiology of Fear and Panic Attacks

There is a great deal of information being imparted in this first session, probably more than in subsequent ones. In order to make the imparting of this information as lively and interactive as possible, I ask the client a number of questions as we go along. Then I build on and elaborate on his or her responses with the information that follows. The first question is, "Is anxiety a good thing or a bad thing?" Building on his or her responses, I point out three important aspects of anxiety:

- It alerts people to danger.

- It is a basic motivating force.

- It can make people aware of problems and conflicts, which they may have buried or denied.

Hence, anxiety is useful in daily functioning and helps people survive. It is part of life, which is why the goal is never to *remove* anxiety. However, anxiety can also be excessive, as in panic disorder, and then the goal is to challenge it and channel it so that it works for rather than against the client.

The second question is: "What *is* a panic attack, aside from the symptoms; what produces it, what is taking place?" (Use the answers given to lead into the following material.) "In order to understand panic, we need to first understand fear."

Fear: The Fight/Flight Response: When confronted with imminent, life-threatening danger, the organism responds with the fight/flight response. Such an alarm response is present in any organism that has a sensory system and can move, so that it can attempt to save itself when in danger.

When threat is perceived, the autonomic nervous system (i.e., the part of the nervous system not under our voluntary control) becomes activated. And specifically, the branch of the autonomic nervous system that is responsible for arousing the body and getting it ready for fighting or fleeing is the sympathetic nervous system. "What are the parts of the body where you need sudden, increased strength?" (Elicit responses.) It is the big muscles in the arms and legs. "What two ingredients create rapid strength?" These are oxygen and glucose, i.e., sugar. We get the oxygen through breathing, and glucose is released from the liver into the bloodstream. The blood must quickly reach the big muscles, delivering oxygen and glucose to the tissues. This means that the heart has a big job to do. It must pump hard and fast to redistribute the blood in the body. This also means that there will be less blood flow to other parts of the body, e.g., skin, hands and feet, and the gastrointestinal system. "What happens if there is less blood flow to the hands and feet?" They may feel cold, tingly, and numb. It simply means that there is less blood flow to those parts of the body. "As we go along, think of the symptoms you have during a panic attack."

As mentioned earlier, the lungs work harder to bring in the extra oxygen. There are other changes, e.g., sweating. "What function would sweating serve?" Primarily to cool down the body. The pupils dilate to increase the visual field, in case there is further danger. The blood coagulates faster, making it less likely for the person to bleed to death.

These are the *physiological* changes that take place in order to prepare the organism for the fight/flight response. The *mental* changes are that attention is narrowly focused on the danger. In fact, the person is so alert to the danger that, as a consequence, many other events taking place at the moment are ignored. The *behavioral* changes involve running, in which case fear is probably the dominant emotion, and fighting, in which case anger and aggression must be mustered up for the person to fight effectively.

The sympathetic nervous system also stimulates the release of *adrenaline* and *noradrenaline* from the adrenal medulla. These hormones have essentially the same effect as the sympathetic nervous system, further increasing the above-mentioned changes, so that the arousal lasts for a while. These hormones and the sympathetic nervous system can also substitute for each other if one is damaged or dysfunctional.

"Now, do you wonder if this arousal in the body could escalate indefinitely? Have you feared that anxiety will go on and on, without ending?" This does not occur. First, the parasympathetic nervous system, the other branch of the autonomic nervous system, will kick in, counteracting the sympathetic nervous system activity. The parasympathetic nervous system is responsible for restoring the body to a more relaxed state. In addition, eventually other hormones are released into the blood that will destroy adrenaline and noradrenaline. However, this does not occur right away, which is why the person is keyed up for a while.

The Connection Between the Fight/Flight Response and Panic: "Now you may ask yourself what all this has to do with panic. After all, you do not have someone pointing a gun at you or a hungry tiger ready to devour you." The sympathetic nervous system does not get triggered only in situations of life-threatening danger. It gets triggered with emotional upheaval, sudden injury, etc. Think of a smoke detector or car alarm. "Would you want them to be set a little too high or too low?" If too high, a potential fire or theft might be well in progress before the alarm sounds. If too low, any slight vapor from cooking or someone bumping against the car could set the alarm off. The ideal would be a perfect system, but life is not perfect. "Now, if not perfectly set, would you want the fight/flight response set a little too low or too high?" Obviously it is better if set a little low. Since it has to do with survival, you would not want to miss potential danger, even if this means that there will be a few false alarms along the way.

Another aspect to look at is the complexity of the human creature, who considers many things as vital to their life and well-being, e.g., social approval. "I have to carry off this speaking engagement well or I'll feel incompetent and dumb." "I absolutely must pass this exam or I won't get the job." In other words, people view many things besides physical survival as "dangerous" or at least potentially harmful to their lives.

The Difference Between Panic and a Fear Reaction: There is one significant difference between panic attacks and fear reactions. When confronted with life-threatening danger, the person will have prepared him or herself for high activity—running or fighting. In panic, since there is no outside threat, this high activity does not take place. This creates an imbalance. The oxygen supply is now in excess of the metabolic rate. Too much oxygen intake creates the paradoxical contrast of too little oxygen reaching the tissues, which in the brain produces sensations of light-headedness, dizziness, feelings of unreality, and blurred vision. (Breathing will be expanded upon in the next chapter.)

Skill Building

Breaking Down Panic, Fear, and Anxiety into Their Components

When a panicker first comes in for treatment, he or she usually feels no control over the panic event. With treatment, most clients will be able to exercise varying amounts of control, but first they must separate out the different parts of this response. Hence, it is exceedingly useful to view the panic attack as a process, consisting of physiological, cognitive, and behavioral components.

"It is very useful to learn to look at a panic attack by breaking it down to its components, whether a physiological (physical), a cognitive (thoughts and images), or a behavioral (actions observable to the outsider) manifestation. If you learn to break down panic and anxiety reactions, you will increasingly be able to intervene at different points along the panic process. Let's look at an example. I will break down one event into steps. Tell me if each sentence reflects a physiological, cognitive, or behavioral component." (Write this up on a blackboard, easel, or have your client look at it in the client manual, session 1.)

Example:	Component:
I went to a department store. While there, I suddenly felt like a panic was coming on, and I felt hot.	P
What if I fainted? I'd feel so embarrassed.	C
I went to look for the exit.	B
But then I just decided to stay close to the exit rather than leave the store; I thought that the panic might go away.	B and C
After a while I felt so bad that I decided to leave.	B

"This example and the other one in your book should give you a good idea what the task is. I will ask you to dissect in this way each panic you have in the coming two to three weeks using Worksheet 3: The Components of a Panic Attack (at the end of this session). Separate out each part of the panic on a different line and identify it as being physiological, cognitive, or behavioral. If you don't have a panic attack this week, you can use the worksheet when approaching a phobic situation, if you have phobias. You can also use it to describe a worry you might have this week, especially if it makes you feel anxious. The principle is the same and you need to practice on it this week.

"Please fill out two samples of this worksheet this coming week. If truly nothing comes up, break down two panic attacks from your past memory, but indicate how long ago they occurred. They will not be as accurate as current recordings."

Session Summary

"Let's review what we learned today. We have gone over how panic is related to the fight/flight response. In the fight/flight response, all the symptoms have a meaning or a purpose. Quick and drastic changes take place in the cardiovascular system, breathing, sweat glands, and other physical systems. The mind gets very narrowly focused, and the behavior is often that of fleeing or fighting. The challenge for you is to apply this knowledge to your panic experiences. Rather than fearing the symptoms, can you start to apply a bit of what you learned today? That is, next time you have a panic-related symptom, can you describe what is happening in your body, mind, and behavior that is related to the fight/flight response?

"We also went over Worksheet 2, where you will start recording helpful coping behaviors and statements, and Worksheet 3, which will help you break down the panic into its components."

This is a good time to emphasize again that the tools you offer are geared toward overcoming the fear of panics. For example, "Today and in the remaining sessions you will acquire information and learn strategies to challenge and cope with panics. That is, the treatment is aimed toward *overcoming the fear of panic attacks*. If you reach a point where you have no fear whatsoever, the panics usually go away. We will be monitoring this fear via the SUDS scale in Worksheet 1 and the PACQ. Your part will be to do the homework. Remember, most of the learning will occur through the homework you do between the sessions."

Feedback From Client

"What questions, aside from what you brought up earlier, do you have about what we reviewed today? Are there any related issues you wish to address?"

Difficulties You May Encounter

Your Client Has Not Filled Out the Self-Rating Scales and Worksheets

Your client may come back saying that he or she did not have the time, forgot it, or thought it was not important enough. It looks like resistance, but exactly why? The reasons for this may be varied. Some clients believe their problem is "medical" and see little value in homework. Others have an image and corresponding expectations of traditional psychotherapy, where they get to say what is on their minds and the therapist listens and makes interpretations. In this latter setting there is usually no homework, and certainly no scales and worksheets to fill out. Some people have great dependency needs and are helpless to take initiative on their own. Others again have unexpressed anger and resist as a result of it. Finally, there are others who have a sense of entitlement and the view, "I'll do it when I feel like it."

It helps to explore what lies behind this resistance, but you may not have time to do it all in this first treatment session. In that case you can postpone it to the next session (and let the client know you will do so). These issues may come up at any time during treatment. After exploring them, you may want to go over again why homework is so important.

"The main reasons for homework assignments are:

- It will allow both of us to monitor your progress closely. I may not be able to tell exactly how you are doing, and you might not think of telling me how you have been feeling or doing in different areas. It allows me to observe more closely what is going on.

- One of the steps toward recovery is for you to become a *participant-observer*. Rather than feel that you are carried away by a wave of fear, you will observe yourself and thereby learn more about yourself and how to master fear.

- Homework is an integral part of the kind of therapy I do, cognitive-behavior therapy. Research has shown that people who do their homework consistently and well have a better treatment outcome. Our goal is also for you to function independently of me. The more skills you learn and master, the more control you will have over your progress. Reading and working on your worksheets and exposures is a big part of acquiring those skills."

"But Why Do I Have Panic Disorder?"

In spite of the material reviewed so far, your client still wants definitive answers. Here is a sample dialogue:

Client: But why do I have panic disorder?

Therapist: In any one person's case, one cannot be absolutely certain. Is there anything we've covered so far that you think can give potential answers?

(If your client gives a meaningful answer, you may just reinforce it as a likely combination of biological, psychological, and stress factors. Let's assume here that your client gives a vague answer.)

Therapist: Today we went over the fight/flight response, which occurs quite often outside of imminently life-threatening situations. Research has shown that people who develop fear of panics and thus panic disorder may have a biological predisposition, psychological vulnerabilities, and a significant stressor that makes the vulnerabilities manifest in the form of symptoms and fear.

Client: But I did not have this before. It just happened.

Therapist: I wish I had all the answers, but I don't. The same could be said about a person getting very depressed without a big bad event having taken place. He or she might also never have been seriously depressed before. But let's look at this. We sometimes don't know in advance about a biological predisposition. But what about a psychological one? Has your life been relatively easy, or have you had to deal with major life issues?

(If the client has, you might say:)

Therapist: Maybe it's surprising that something like panic disorder has not manifested before. Let's also look at precipitating stressors. Did anything very stressful occur prior to your first panic? As you can see, it is quite complex.

Homework

The homework for session 2 is as follows:

1. Worksheet 1: Panic Frequency and Intensity.

2. Start to write a helpful statement or a behavior onto Worksheet 2: My Personal Coping Affirmations.

3. Read session 1 in your client manual and bring up any questions or comments.

4. Fill out two samples of Worksheet 3: The Components of a Panic Attack.

If agoraphobia is present:

5. In the beginning of the session we went over your sample of Worksheet 9: Goal and the Steps to Achieve It. I would like you to think of other goals regarding phobias that you might have and work with them. Remember to set goals you are likely to reach in our remaining thirteen to fifteen sessions. Use one sheet for each separate goal. I will be comparing them with the fears stated in the SESA, which you filled out.

6. We will be talking in greater detail about phobias later, but I want to ask you to work on some exposures right away. That is, do something you have been avoiding because of fear. These exposures need to pose a challenge—they should be somewhat difficult in order for you to benefit from them, but not too difficult to do. I would like you to think of exposures you can do *at least* three days this coming week, but the more days you do exposures, the better. Please record them now onto Worksheet 10: Your Weekly Exposures, where it says "Planned Exposures." You can write the steps to be taken under "Steps" and the distance, time, and/or number of attempts this week in the space next to it. Leave the "Goal" part blank for now. I will also be recording your exposures so as not to forget what assignments we agreed on. (You, the therapist, will be recording the client's exposures in Therapist Record 10T: Tracking Client's Weekly Exposures.) Record what you ended up doing under "Actual Effort" and let me now what you've recorded there in our next session. Your plans and effort should ideally be the same. On occasion something may come up that prevents you from doing what you planned. In that case try to do another exposure and note it also under "Actual Effort." You can always do more than you agreed on. I will also record what you actually did in the next session to keep track of how you are doing with your assignments.

If the client has difficulty deciding on exposures, help him or her based on phobias mentioned during the assessment or what you saw in the measuring scales.

Worksheet 2: My Personal Coping Affirmations

1. *Don't bolt! I will stay put and continue doing what I was doing, even if it is hard.*

2. _____

3. _____

4. _____

5. _____

6. _____

7. _____

8. _____

9. _____

10. _____

Worksheet 3: The Components of a Panic Attack

Event/Situation: _____ Date: _____ Put each component of the specific panic attack or fearful event on a separate line.	State if P, C, B: Physiological, Cognitive, or Behavioral
1. _____	
2. _____	
3. _____	
4. _____	
5. _____	
6. _____	
7. _____	

Event/Situation: _____ Date: _____ Put each component of the specific panic attack or fearful event on a separate line.	State if P, C, B: Physiological, Cognitive, or Behavioral
1. _____	
2. _____	
3. _____	
4. _____	
5. _____	
6. _____	
7. _____	

Session 2

Breathing Retraining

Monitoring of Current Status

Review Worksheet 1: Panic Frequency and Intensity. Proceed as in session 1.

Agenda

This session follows logistically the previous one. In session 1 you covered the physiology of fear and anxiety. Your client learned that the symptoms he or she fears so much in panic are natural and necessary changes when aroused with fear. Now you will have the client take an overbreathing test to induce acute hyperventilation, but it is best not to label it hyperventilation at this time, so as not to arouse unnecessary fear. This test is likely to bring on some of the symptoms your client experiences in a panic. If it does, it can show your client right away how easily the feared symptoms can be induced. You substantiate the experience with an elaboration of the physiology of breathing and hyperventilation.

After describing the four ways to stop hyperventilation, you will expand upon and teach diaphragmatic breathing, which is the best of these methods.

Review of Homework

The homework assignments that you are following up since session 1 are:

1. Worksheet 1: Panic Frequency and Intensity

2. Worksheet 2: My Personal Coping Affirmations. (One or two entries.)

3. Reading session 1 in the client manual. (Spend a little time reviewing highlights of the fight/flight response, and see if your client has been able to integrate the material.)

4. Two samples of Worksheet 3: The Components of a Panic Attack.

If agoraphobia is present:

5. Agoraphobic goals as reflected in Worksheet 9: Goal and the Steps to Achieve It (one for each goal).

6. Exposures as recorded on Worksheet 10: Your Weekly Exposures, under "Actual Effort." Write down your client's exposures onto Therapist Record 10T: Tracking Client's Weekly Exposures, under "Actual Effort." (Ask the client—unless he or she volunteers—what exact steps were taken and how many times, distance, etc.) You may want to set new homework assignments regarding *in vivo* exposures now while you are at it. It is logistically easier, especially since this is so closely tied in to the report you are getting back and since you both have the forms in front of you. (I usually plan the other assignments at the end.)

Concepts and Skills

Psychoeducation

Overbreathing Test

What you need: A timer or a watch or clock with a second hand.

Instructions (Description of task and exclusionary criteria):
"Today we are going to work on diaphragmatic breathing, but before we start, let's do an overbreathing test. While this test is in itself harmless, some people should be excluded from doing it, in case a physical condition is in any way exacerbated by this exercise. If you have epileptic or other seizures, chronic arrythmia, heart or lung problems, moderate to severe asthma, a history of fainting, extremely low blood pressure, or if you are pregnant, let me know. Do you fall into any of these categories?"

"Please stand up. First, let's practice a bit. I will demonstrate a few times and will then ask you to try it."

While standing opposite your client, demonstrate a breathing pattern like panting but a bit slower, breathing deeply—in and out through the mouth, exaggerating the exhale.

"Try to make a sound like I did, when you exhale. Make it strong enough so that I can hear it."

Have the client take three to five breaths this way. Demonstrate again if it is not done correctly.

"Good! Now we will do it for one-and-a-half minutes. I'll do it with you. Pay attention to any sensations that you may feel while doing this, or right after. If you can't stand the sensations, you can stop earlier, but try to feel the sensations and stay with them for the full time, if you can."

After the test, ask the client to describe any sensations that were felt and whether or not they were similar to the sensations in a panic. If no sensations were experienced, the client either did not do it correctly or needs to do it longer. (Sometimes, up to three minutes are needed for the full experience of the sensations.) After the overbreathing test go over the physiology of breathing and hyperventilation.

The Physiology of Breathing and Hyperventilation

Our lungs breathe in air and the hemoglobin in the blood carries the oxygen to the tissues, where the cells use the oxygen in their metabolism. As a by-product of this metabolism, carbon dioxide is produced and carried back by the blood to the lungs, where it is exhaled. When the breathing exceeds metabolic need—that is, when one breathes more than is needed at the time, the person is overbreathing. This may lead to hyperventilation.

In hyperventilation, there is excess exhalation of carbon dioxide. The loss of carbon dioxide makes the blood more alkalinic and less acidic. This change results in oxygen being more tightly bound to the hemoglobin, and this, together with vascular constriction (tightening of the blood vessels), means that less oxygen is being released to the tissues. Diminished oxygen to the brain produces sensations of dizziness, light-headedness, faint feelings, blurred vision, and feelings of unreality. Diminished oxygen to the extremities results in tingling, numbness, and cold sensations. If this continues, eventually the kidneys will compensate to suppress the symptoms.

How Do You Know If Your Client Is a Chronic Overbreather?

Some people overbreathe much of the time as a result of general stress and anxiety or bad breathing habits. Overbreathing can take place subtly, which is why hyperventilation may go unrecognized. Some give away signs are: shallow breathing with the upper chest expanding, breathing through the mouth, breathing at a rate of eighteen or more breaths per minute while relaxed, sighing, gasping for air, yawning, frequent clearing of the throat, and heavy breathing. The paradox is that while the person is taking in too much air, he or she has the sensation of getting too little air. The logical response then is to try to breathe harder to get more air, but this only makes the hyperventilation worse.

Skill Building

How to Stop Hyperventilation

There are four ways to stop hyperventilation:

1. *Holding your breath*
   "Let's assume you have a panic tomorrow and you have not learned diaphragmatic breathing. What can you do to stop possible hyperventilation and slow down your symptoms? You can hold your breath a few times in a row for as long as you feel comfortable, maybe ten to fifteen seconds. That

is, hold your breath, take a breath, hold your breath again, and so forth. Why do you think this may work?" (Elicit answers.) "It is because it temporarily prevents the dissipation of carbon dioxide."

2. *Breathing in and out of a paper bag*

   "If you have gone to an emergency room for panics, you may have been told to do this. Why do you think this works?" (Elicit answers.) "The carbon dioxide is in the bag and is breathed back in. Now, you can't do this everywhere. For instance, you are not driving safely if you try at the same time to hold a bag to your mouth and nose. And you would probably not sit in a meeting at work or in a classroom breathing into a bag."

3. *Vigorous exercise*

   "You could run up and down stairs, do aerobics in place, run, walk briskly, and so on. Why does this work? You will breathe in (and out) a great deal, but in this case the metabolism is quickly increased to produce more energy, so the oxygen taken in will be used up, and a larger quantity of carbon dioxide is produced. Again, you cannot do this while driving, or in many other places. Vigorous exercise and breathing into a bag can be done at home."

4. *Deep diaphragmatic breathing*

   "This is the best way to stop hyperventilation. It allows you to use the full capacity of your lungs. However, let me make a point. Even if you are not a hyperventilator, this is the best means I know of helping your body to slow down and diminish the symptoms in a panic. Therefore, it is a very useful coping skill for most people."

(The instructions for diaphragmatic breathing follow.)

Breathing Retraining

Diaphragmatic breathing is a very useful coping tool. If your client hyperventilates in a panic, diaphragmatic breathing can have a direct impact on the symptoms. Likewise, the more the client learns to do it on a regular basis, the more likely that he or she can stop chronic hyperventilation. Indirectly, the breathing can slow down the other physical events in a panic.

Instructions

Ask your client to stand up again and instruct him or her to take a deep breath in and out. Watch for signs of lifting the rib cage and shoulders, breathing quickly, and having the mouth open. Now demonstrate how to do diaphragmatic breathing while standing; then have your client try it. Most people find this hard to do, unless they have already learned it.

Subsequently, I explain diaphragmatic breathing while demonstrating by leaning back in my armchair so that I can get as close as possible to a lying-down position. I place a pillow (or a folded jacket) on my diaphragm/stomach and demonstrate the following steps:

1. Lie on your back on a bed or carpeted floor without a pillow or with a thin one. Instead of placing the pillow under your head, place two or three pillows on your stomach/diaphragm. Watch the top of the pillows. When you

breathe *in*, your diaphragm/stomach should expand (to allow for the extra air), thus *raising the pillows.* When you breathe *out,* the pillows should move down again. It helps to exaggerate the movement of your diaphragm, especially while learning the technique. Breathe slowly in and out through your *nose,* not through your mouth. (The only exceptions are if you have a bad cold, asthma, or something impeding the air flow through your nostrils. In that case, keep your mouth open only a little and allow the same amount of air to flow in and out.)

2. Lying on your back as described above, discard the pillows and place your hand over your waist and navel. Look at the ceiling or close your eyes. Proceed as above. This time feel your stomach rising up and falling down with your hand.

3. Lying on your back as above, place your arms at your sides. Look at the ceiling or close your eyes. Proceed as in step 1. Focus on your diaphragm/stomach, and *feel* it move up and down. I like to think of it as "becoming one with my breathing."

4. Sit on a sofa, leaning back, so that you can watch your stomach area. Watch your diaphragm/stomach move up as you breathe in, down as you breathe out.

5. Sit straight up and breathe in and out while your stomach moves out and in (that is, your breathing and your stomach move in opposite directions). As in steps 1 through 4, make sure that your upper chest and shoulders are perfectly still.

6. Stand up and do the same as in step 5.

7. Remember to breathe through your nose. At rest, nasal breathing is more efficient. Practice breathing this way as slowly as possible, ideally between eight and twelve breaths per minute; generally, the slower the breathing the better.

8. Breathe in slowly and then out slowly. Either breathe out a bit slower than breathing in or breathe out at the same pace and hold a little while before taking your next breath. Hold at the end of the breathing-out cycle only for as long as you feel comfortable. The more you practice, the more you will feel comfortable in slowing down your breathing. (Do *not* take in a breath and then hold unnaturally before breathing out.)

9. Practice twice a day for five minutes. Do this daily.

I emphasize the need to start practicing by lying down, since it is very difficult to learn this type of breathing while standing. If a client does very poorly when I follow up on the breathing technique in the third session, I specifically inquire whether he or she practiced lying down. More often than not, the client tried to skip this step.

Session Summary

"The overbreathing test we did brought on some symptoms, some of which reminded you of panic symptoms. Then we went over the physiology of breathing and hyperventilation, which explains why and how the symptoms are produced. We went over the four ways to stop hyperventilation. The best one is diaphragmatic breathing, which I demonstrated and you tried out."

Feedback from Client

"What questions, aside from what you brought up earlier, do you have about what we reviewed today? Are there any related issues you wish to address?"

Difficulties You May Encounter

Your Client Has Filled Out Only One Sample of Worksheet 9

If agoraphobia is an issue, make sure that you review closely what your client did with the first sample of Worksheet 9 (Goal and the Steps to Achieve It). If time is lacking, ask to borrow the worksheet (or copy it). It is important that your client understand the task. I have had clients who used it for their weekly exposures, essentially instead of Worksheet 10. This is not its purpose. The client should plan on goals as soon as possible and use them as guides. This can be particularly useful when they get discouraged with a particular task.

The Hyperventilation Scared Your Client

Client: This is really scary, just like in a panic. I didn't like it!

Therapist: It is very understandable that you would not like the sensations produced. However, think of it this way: Your reaction may suggest that hyperventilation is a component in your panic attacks. The hyperventilation is quite easy to stop with diaphragmatic breathing. This simple method can help you control several panic symptoms rather quickly. Wouldn't that make you feel a bit hopeful?

Client: Yes.

Homework

The homework for Treatment Session 3 is as follows:

1. Worksheet 1: Panic Frequency and Intensity.

2. Read session 2 in your client manual and bring up any questions or comments.

3. I would like you to fill out one (or two if the client did not do well the previous week) additional samples of Worksheet 3: The Components of a Panic Attack. Dissect either a panic attack, a phobic encounter or anticipating a phobic exposure, or another experience of worry and anxiety.

4. Learn diaphragmatic breathing by practicing five minutes twice a day, daily, until we meet again. In the next session, I will ask you to demonstrate it for me.

If agoraphobia is present:

5. Exposures (for the client to record on Worksheet 10 and you on Therapist Record 10T, under "Planned Exposures"). This homework was probably set in the beginning of the session.

Right after the session, while fresh on your mind, you may wish to fill out Therapist Record 9T: Tracking Goal Progress, which can be found on page 158. This form is simpler than it seems at first glance. It is designed for an individual or a group session, so in this case you write down only your client's name. With only one client, you have the luxury of placing each goal of the client in a separate square (in a group, you abbreviate all the goals of a given client into one square). For each week, check off whether or not your client made progress *vis-á-vis* a particular goal. This allows you to easily track progress on all fronts and prompts your client to plan assignments in regards to neglected goals.

Session 3

The Calming Breath, Identifying Negative Automatic Thoughts

Monitoring of Current Status

Review Worksheet 1: Panic Frequency and Intensity. Proceed as in session 1.

Agenda

In this session you will follow up on diaphragmatic breathing: how well your client has learned it and the difficulties encountered. You will go over how to apply it to everyday life, and how to eventually use it in high anxiety and panic situations.

While sessions 1 and 2 dealt primarily with the physiological component of panic, at the end of this session you will introduce the cognitive component. Although the actual cognitive restructuring starts in session 4, you need to lay the groundwork for it. Your client will learn to recognize negative automatic thoughts, and more than that, identify very *specific* thoughts.

Review of Homework

The homework assignments that you are following up since session 2 are:

1. Worksheet 1: Panic Frequency and Intensity.

2. Read session 2 in the client manual.

3. One (or two) samples from Worksheet 3: The Components of a Panic Attack.

4. Practice diaphragmatic breathing.
"Let's stand up and show me how you're doing with the diaphragmatic breathing." You will get a good idea if he or she has practiced, and you may need to make some corrections. If your client is doing poorly and/or did not go through all the steps (especially lying down), briefly go over those steps again. If needed, ask the client to practice more, and say that you will continue monitoring his or her progress.

If agoraphobia is present:

5. Exposures as recorded on Worksheet 10: Your Weekly Exposures, under "Actual Effort." Plan new exposures with your client.

Concepts and Skills

You want to be certain that your client masters the basics of diaphragmatic breathing before expanding its use. If your client had problems with it, look at the end of this chapter on ways to approach various difficulties.

Skill Building

Expanding Diaphragmatic Breathing to Everyday Life

"Start now to pay attention to your breathing during the day: sitting at work, watching TV, and so on. Do this by asking yourself, 'How am I breathing right now?' Take a couple of minutes then to do diaphragmatic breathing. You may wish to place a reminder in places like the refrigerator door or your desk to make sure you will keep working on it.

"Once you are able to do diaphragmatic breathing more often in your everyday life, you can start to apply it when you feel anxious, feel a panic attack coming on, or in the middle of one. This will work only if you practice diligently. You know from experience that in a panic it is very difficult to concentrate and think constructively. In other words, you can apply it to high anxiety and panic situations only if you have already learned it well."

The follow-up on the breathing may span over a couple of more sessions. Most clients learn it in two to four weeks and find it quite useful.

Psychoeducation

Identifying Negative Thoughts in Panic and Phobic Situations

Thoughts have power. Some people recognize their thoughts for what they are: just thoughts that come and go. Others become fearful of their thoughts. In panic disorder, the thought that a panic attack may lead to a stroke can become an ingrained thought, which can dominate the person's thinking. It may become an automatic thought. (More on automatic thoughts in the next chapter.)

Thoughts play a central role in bringing on a panic attack. If a person believes that something outside or within is a threat to his or her safety or life, the process of the panic can begin. For example, the person might feel tightness in the chest, which may be an uncomfortable sensation in itself. Next, how the sensation is interpreted may determine whether or not a panic attack will come on. If the sensation is interpreted in a neutral way, it is unlikely that a panic will ensue. Conversely, if it is interpreted as catastrophic, there is a much higher likelihood of panicking. These fearful thoughts are commonly called automatic thoughts because they occur so easily, automatically, often outside of one's awareness.

Distinguishing Between Feelings and Thoughts: Before getting started on thoughts and how to challenge them, your client needs to distinguish between feelings and thoughts. Many people have a hard time making the distinction. Give your client a few examples:

- I feel sad. Is it a feeling or a thought? (Feeling)

- I feel people should be able to express their opinion. (Thought)

- I feel that he is unfair. (Thought)

- (In a panic) I feel I'm going to faint. (Thought)

The last example is a thought because people hardly ever faint in panic. The sensations of dizziness, light-headedness, unreality, etc., in a panic have nothing to do with fainting.

Feelings can be expressed in *one word*, e.g., "I feel loving, sad, disappointed, angry, scared, guilty, ashamed, lonely, happy, unhappy, mad, furious, jealous, hurt, frustrated, insecure, irritated, tense, suspicious, content, jittery, excited, afraid, joyful." If a person starts a sentence with "I feel that . . . ," the word "that" is usually a lead-in to a thought. Expressions such as "I feel that he is unfair" are often accompanied by emotions, but that expression is a thought. To sum, the two give-aways to thoughts are "I feel" followed by "that," and the more words are used, the more likely that a thought, rather than a feeling, is being expressed.

Skill Building

Identifying *Specific* Automatic Thoughts

One of your tasks as a therapist is to train your client to become aware of *specific* automatic thoughts. Phrases such as "I'm going to have a heart attack," "I'll die of suffocation," "I'll faint" are quite specific and therefore lend themselves well to challenging. Thoughts like "I'll lose control," "I'm going crazy," "Something awful will happen" are too general because they mean different things to different people. Ask your client also to translate questions into *specific statements or predictions*, e.g., "I will die from a heart attack" instead of "What if I die?" Worksheet 3: The Components of a Panic Attack can help your client look at his or her thoughts in panic and other high-anxiety situations and recognize if the thoughts are general or specific.

Questions and strategies that help bring about specific automatic thoughts in panic and phobic situations are:

1. What exactly do you mean by _____ (going crazy, losing control, being unable to control the car)?

2. How would _____ (you die, stop breathing)?

3. What exactly are you afraid will happen if _____ (your heart skips a beat, you become light-headed)? Do you have an image?

4. What is the *worst* that you think could happen if _____ (you couldn't leave the meeting, the feeling didn't go away)? Ask for thoughts or images.

5. Have your client close his or her eyes and imagine being in the middle of a "bad" panic. Ask, "Why is it bad? What do you think will happen in that moment?"

6. Have your client imagine approaching a fearful situation or doing a feared activity. Ask, "Why don't you want to proceed? Something is holding you back. Remember, right now it does not matter if it is rational or not. We need to understand what exactly is holding you back."

7. Give your client the instructions to approach a real phobic situation (if your client is phobic) and then ask himself or herself, "Why exactly don't I want to do this right now?"

8. Tell your clients to pay attention when and if they suddenly become anxious. Tell them to ask themselves what were they thinking right before they noticed the anxiety. Have them try to recreate any thoughts or images.

Linking Triggers to Automatic Thoughts

"Worksheet 4: Challenging Automatic Thoughts is a very useful thought record to target the fear elicited in panic attacks and phobic situations."(Very similar approaches can be used to alter other negative automatic thoughts, such as those related to depression and anger.) "Later you will learn to challenge the automatic thoughts. Worksheet 4 is not easy to learn, it requires some effort. You will learn it in steps. Hence, you will work on half of the worksheet first to make it easier to later move to the full one-page worksheet.

"In this first half of the worksheet, you need to link the specific automatic thoughts to the trigger. In regards to both the trigger and the automatic thought (numbers 2 and 3), don't use general words such as 'panic' or 'anxiety,' but *exactly what* about the panic triggered your fear (stated in number 2), and *exactly what* you feared might happen *as a result of the panic sensations* (stated in number 3)."

Instructions

"Use Worksheet 4: Challenging Automatic Thoughts, 1st Step whenever you experience a full-blown panic attack, a more limited attack, or encounter another anxiety-producing situation, such as a fearful sensation or situation. The instructions follow the worksheet. As the instructions show, you must learn to distinguish between the *trigger*, i.e., a panic sensation or a phobic situation (the 'Specific Trigger,' listed under #2) on one hand, and the feared *consequence* (the 'Automatic Thought,' listed under #3) on the other hand. It doesn't matter if your thoughts make sense or not. Even if they seem illogical, they need to be worked on. A final point: Use *as few words as possible* when you fill out the worksheet. The more words you use, the more complicated you will make your task."

Summary of Session

"Today we reviewed your breathing skills. As you become better at it, you will find it to be a powerful way to master your body's reactions when anxious. We also discussed the importance of thoughts and how to distinguish between feelings and thoughts.

"Before you can challenge and change your negative thoughts, you need to be able to identify what the exact thoughts are. If you have not been fully aware of them, there are ways to bring those specific thoughts to the forefront. We reviewed Worksheet 4, 1st Step to help you pay very close attention to the triggers and exact thoughts."

Feedback from Client

"What questions, aside from what you brought up earlier, do you have about what we reviewed today? Are there any related issues you wish to address?"

Difficulties You May Encounter Regarding Diaphragmatic Breathing

Feeling Light-headed or As If Not Getting Enough Air

This is experienced particularly by clients who are chronic overbreathers. They are likely to experience symptoms off and on. It is helpful to review again the physiology of breathing and hyperventilation. Sustained hyperventilation elicits renal compensation, so that the symptoms are suppressed. However, any *change* in breathing can bring on the symptoms again, because the balance is precarious. Another possibility is that your client is just not doing it correctly and/or gets very anxious paying attention to their breathing. Encourage your client to continue practicing. Practice brings mastery.

Not Able to Get a Rhythm Going or Unable to Breathe Slowly Enough

First, make sure your client is not holding his or her breath after the inhalation, but simply proceeds to exhale when it comes naturally. Sometimes, clients benefit from counting to produce a steady rhythm. The person can be instructed to count one, two, three seconds breathing in; one, two, three, four seconds breathing out. This can be practiced a number of times. Next, the client can slow down further by counting one, two, three, four seconds breathing in; and one, two, three, four seconds breathing out, and holding for a bit. This can be repeated a number of times.

Your client can slow down the rate by adding one second breathing in and one second breathing out until he or she feels comfortable. This can be practiced for several days. If your client wishes to, he or she can check the time and see if they are able to breathe from eight to twelve breaths per minute at rest.

Unable to Do Diaphragmatic Breathing Sitting Straight or Standing

If the person can do the first steps, then it is only a matter of time until he or she can learn the others. Have your client continue to practice while lying down until he or she is very comfortable with it. Then your client can practice slouching back and slowly sitting progressively straighter. When sitting straight is mastered, it should not be too difficult to do the technique standing up.

Homework

The homework for session 4 is as follows:

1. Worksheet 1: Panic Frequency and Intensity.

2. Read session 3 in the client manual and bring up any questions or comments.

3. Continue working on diaphragmatic breathing: Off and on during the day, pay attention to your breathing and apply diaphragmatic breathing. Start to apply it to high anxiety and panic situations. Please report on your progress in doing so.

4. Fill out two samples of Worksheet 4: Challenging Automatic Thoughts, 1st Step. If you have no panic attack or phobic encounter this week, practice with any experience that produces worry and anxiety. (Ask your client to make you copies of his or her samples of the worksheet for future reference.)

If agoraphobia is present:

5. Exposures (for the client to record on Worksheet 10 and you on Therapist Record 10T, under "Planned Exposures"). This homework was probably set in the beginning of the session.

Worksheet 4: Challenging Automatic Thoughts, 1st Step

1. Date.

_____

2. Specific Trigger: **Situation and/or physical symptom.**

_____

3. Automatic Thought (Negative Thought). **The *exact* bad thing that will happen if you feel or do** (write #2 here): _____
   is:

   How strongly do you believe your Automatic Thought will happen, 0–100%? _____

Instructions to Worksheet 4: Challenging Automatic Thoughts, 1st Step

1. Date. By always recording the date, you will be able to monitor your progess over time.

_____

2. Specific Trigger: Situation (driving over the bridge, going to the mall) and/or physical symptoms (dizziness, tightness in chest, numbness in arms). What brought on your fear thought (Automatic Thought)? (Don't write "panic" or "anxiety," but what specifically in the panic or anxiety made you afraid.)

_____

3. Automatic Thought (Negative Thought). **The *exact* bad thing that will happen if you feel or do** (write #2 here): _____
   is: The thought should be stated in the form of a specific theory/prediction (not as a question, e.g., "I will have a heart attack and die," not "Will I have a heart attack and die?")
   Questions to guide you: What are you afraid might happen with these symptoms? What's the worst thing that you think will happen in this situation?

   How strongly do you believe your Automatic Thought will happen, 0–100% _____

   0=You do not believe the Automatic Thought will happen (in which case there should be no Automatic Thought).
   50=You're 50% sure that the Automatic Thought will happen.
   100=You're 100% sure the Automatic Thought will happen.
   Use any number between 0 and 100%.

Cognitive Restructuring: Recognizing Cognitive Traps, Challenging Automatic Thoughts

Monitoring of Current Status

Review Worksheet 1: Panic Frequency and Intensity. Proceed as in session 1.

Agenda

Very briefly follow up on diaphragmatic breathing. Inquire whether or not your client has tried to apply it to anxious and panic situations and how successful it has been in helping to decrease the symptoms experienced.

Clients learn in this session that their catastrophic thoughts in panic and phobic situations are indeed very common. They are so common, in fact, that they reflect cognitive traps which are further categorized and labeled. Besides recognizing the specific traps the client resorts to, there are various ways to start challenging them.

You will work next on Worksheet 4: Challenging Automatic Thoughts, the first half of which, "1st Step," you gave to your client as a home assignment. In the first step, the task was to learn to recognize the specific automatic thoughts. Once you have reviewed this first half of the worksheet, you will teach your client how to use the entire worksheet.

Review of Homework

The homework assignments that you are following up since session 3 are:

1. Worksheet 1: Panic Frequency and Intensity.

2. Read session 3 in the client manual.

3. Follow-up on breathing.

4. Two samples of Worksheet 4: Challenging Automatic Thoughts, 1st Step. (Follow up on this home task later in the session when you start to work on the full worksheet. You can use your client's half sheet to illustrate how to fill out the rest of the worksheet.)

If agoraphobia is present:

4. Exposures as recorded on Worksheet 10: Your Weekly Exposures, under "Actual Effort." Plan new exposures with your client.

Concepts and Skills

When a person is anxious, he or she engages in anxious thoughts. These thoughts are an integral part of the panic and phobic experience. They play a role in the development of panic disorder and perhaps an even larger role in the disorder's maintenance.

Real or perceived threat activates cognitive fear structures (also called *schemas*) containing core beliefs and assumptions, which are based on past experiences. People with anxiety disorders show a bias toward seeing danger more readily than the average person and feel at the same time more vulnerable, i.e., less able to cope with the threat. The latter is also based on past experiences. The more caught in the fear cycle, the less the person is able to mobilize more adaptive responses. Obviously, biological and cognitive processes continuously influence each other.

The fearful thoughts are expressed in automatic thoughts, which lie at a more superficial level than core beliefs and assumptions. Automatic thoughts consist of brief statements, images, and memories. Typical automatic thoughts in panic and phobic situations are:

- I'll have a heart attack.

- I may have a stroke.

- I'll lose control.

- I can't breathe; I may suffocate.

How can your client achieve a change in cognitions, especially when the fear structure is so salient? Needless to say, relying on positive self-statements does not work. Socratic dialogue involves asking a series of questions designed to help your client evaluate his or her own thinking. You work together to help direct your client's attention to pertinent issues, and draw the stated hypothesis to its logical conclusion. New hypotheses are pursued. The power lies in the logical argument. Even more powerful is behavioral hypothesis testing, which can be planned to test out the various hypotheses behaviorally.

Understandably, clients often argue their point, defending the possible feared actions that *may* occur (e.g., panic and faint, crash the car, scream at a meeting). One approach here is to again and again return to the previous data (evidence) and point out how their *behavior* actually was under their control at all times. And, if a feared behavior or event ever did take place, was it indeed catastrophic, and did it occur again?

Psychoeducation

You might introduce the subject by saying: "In the last session, we started to work on negative automatic thoughts pertaining to anxious situations and experiences. In fact, we started even earlier, with Worksheet 3. Your task there was to break down panic and other anxious experiences into components: physiological, cognitive, and behavioral.

"Since your task is to overcome the fear associated with panic attacks, we will be targeting these thoughts and beliefs. We will use cognitive (e.g., via Worksheet 4) and behavioral methods to achieve this. And, of course, the diaphragmatic breathing is to help slow down the physical sensations in order to have a sense of control and to more effectively intervene in the anxious response. Hence, we target the fears along several fronts."

Negative Automatic Thoughts Reflect Cognitive Traps

Clients are often convinced that the threatened outcome they fear in panic or phobic situations is a reality. They believe furthermore that this is a unique experience. Instead, your client needs to learn that the event they fear is only a hypothesis, an *erroneous* one, and a common error at that. Cognitive traps always lead the person on a negative path and the person feels worse rather than better. There are two main types of traps: irrational thoughts or cognitive distortions and unhelpful or maladaptive thoughts. (The traps are followed by guidelines on how to challenge them. You can challenge your client when appropriate throughout treatment.)

Irrational Thoughts or Cognitive Distortions: These constitute errors in logic. The following are among the most common cognitive distortions in panic. The first two are emphasized particularly by Barlow and Craske in *Mastery of Your Anxiety and Panic II* (1994). A more extensive list of cognitive distortions is found in *The Feeling Good Handbook* (Burns 1989).

1. **Exaggerating or Overestimating Risk**
   The person greatly exaggerates the odds that a dangerous or bad event will happen and takes it as an established fact. Examples:

   - Next time I panic, I may have a heart attack.

   - I'll lose control in a panic and will create a crash.

   - If I panic, I'll go crazy and hurt others.

   - My throat will close and I'll pass out.

- If I can't control these panicky feelings, they'll get worse and will last forever.

Challenge these erroneous hypotheses using the cognitive technique: Establishing the Facts or Probability vs. Possibility by asking the following types of questions:

- Is this an established fact or is it a hypothesis?

- What objective evidence do you have to substantiate your view that these symptoms are dangerous?

- Is it just *possible* that _____ will happen some day, or is it highly likely to happen in your next panic? What is the percentage of likelihood that the event will happen?

2. Catastrophizing

This is closely related to Overestimating Risk and can take one of two forms:

a. Besides the bad event happening, extreme and horrible consequences will follow. It involves the worst-case scenario and is often expressed in "What if . . . ?" terms. These can take the form of thoughts or images. Examples:

- If I crash the car and die, my children will not have me and they'll be faced with endless misery.

- When I panic, I get scared and upset and my mind gets totally confused. If I keep getting this anxious over little things, it must mean I'm a paranoid schizophrenic.

b. The person underestimates his or her ability to cope with the event. This is often expressed in a negative emotion. Examples:

- If I go out dancing with my friends and have to leave because of panic, I'll be *so embarrassed* I'll never be able to face them again.

- If I leave the store in a panic, I'll *feel humiliated and totally defeated*.

To challenge, use the cognitive technique: Decatastrophizing. This technique involves talking the person through the event. In the case of social fears (e.b., embarrassment), the person may be overestimating the risk, and if it were to take place, exaggerating the severity of it. When such events are anticipated, coping strategies can be used. If the fear is of an extreme consequence, such as serious disasters and death, the person can replay the event over and over in great detail to achieve desensitization, i.e., until the fear response diminishes.

a. Work with a feared image and follow it to completion.

b. Ask the following types of questions: "Is there life after embarrassment? If you saw someone_____ (faint, cry, appear anxious), how would you react and respond?"

3. Control at All Costs

Control is an issue for everyone with panic and phobias. On the one hand a person with panic disorder wants very badly to have control, on the other hand he or she feels out of control. There are two kinds of control here:

a. Control over outside events. Examples:

- I can't stand situations where I'm not in *control*: having to wait for a traffic light to change, sitting in a meeting at work, going to places with others, especially if they are driving.

b. Full control over one's emotions at all times. Examples:

- I should be able to control these panics.
- I may totally lose control; then I'll *go mad*.

To challenge, ask questions about uncertainty and humanness, and distinguishing between what can and what cannot be controlled.

- Can you accept the premise that we cannot predict or control certain things? Or would you want everyone to be able to predict and control everything? What would such a world look like?
- If other people can't predict and control certain things, can you accept that you are the same way?
- Can you learn to distinguish between what you can and what you can't control and put your energy into things that are under your control? For instance, you may not be able to prevent a panic from coming on, but you can certainly learn to respond differently to the attack.
- Do you think it is desirable to live in a world where everyone had such control over their emotions that they would be like robots?

4. Perfectionism or All-or-Nothing Thinking

This cognitive distortion does not show itself so much during the panic attack itself as it helps set the stage for anxiety to flourish. Perfectionists and extremists think in "either/or" terms. They often fall short of the standards they set for themselves. If it is not 100 percent, it is no good. Words such as *always, never, should, must, ought*, and *need to* are often involved. Examples:

- Panic attacks show you are not perfect. There is something definitely wrong with you.
- Everyone else around me is perfectly relaxed and enjoying themselves. If I were not defective with panic disorder, I'd be perfectly normal like they are.

To challenge, use the cognitive technique: Unobtainable Standards vs. Evidence Continuum by asking the following types of questions:

- Can you allow yourself to be human and sometimes imperfect and vulnerable?
- What is the worst that could happen if you are not perfect?
- Draw a line on a piece of paper (see Clark 1989). On one end write "Always perfect job performance," and on the other end "Never perfect job performance." Have the person write down names of family members, friends, and acquaintances and where they would be placed

on the line along this particular dimension. Then have the person place his or her own name on the line. It may help the person see what the norm is, and then question why the rules should not apply to him or her. The same could be done with other areas where the expectations are unreasonable.

5. Emotions/Sensations as Evidence

The person interprets his or her emotions or physical sensations as evidence of reality to the exclusion of more objective evidence. The stronger something is felt, the more it is believed to be a sign of truth. Examples:

- My evidence why I believe I will faint is *the feeling* (i.e., sensation) of lightheadedness and dizziness.

- My evidence for going crazy and ending up in an insane asylum is that I feel so dissociated in a panic. This dissociation will make my mind break down.

To challenge, use the cognitive technique: Establishing the Facts by asking the following types of questions:

- Are feelings good evidence of facts?

- Have your feelings ever been wrong?

- Can physical sensations mean something other than what you are hypothesizing?

Unhelpful or Maladaptive Thoughts: Unlike irrational thoughts, unhelpful thoughts may seem logical and reality-based. They are difficult to dispute with logical reasoning. However, they do not promote well-being. Although maladaptive thoughts may not come up directly in the context of panic attacks, they may be in the background and help to maintain the disorder.

You can test if a thought is maladaptive by asking your client:

- Does this thought make you feel good about yourself?

- Do these thoughts promote your well-being?

1. Disaster Expectation

This is often found in people who worry chronically, which involves a number of panickers. There are three versions of this:

a. The person worries because he or she cannot possibly cope if bad things happen unexpectedly. Therefore, the person takes the stance of always preparing for the worst. Example:

  - I can't let off my guard; I have to worry till they are home safe. Imagine getting a call about them being killed in an accident! That would be unbearable.

b. Magical thinking (this is actually an irrational thought). This means that if the person worries intensely enough, the bad event will not happen. Worrying somehow "saves" them. Few people will admit holding this belief openly, yet I have found it to be extremely common (even among therapists). Examples:

- If I really worry about a disaster happening, it won't happen.

- God will spare me. I paid my dues worrying.

c. Another version of magical thinking is that after many uneventful episodes, the client's luck will run out and the bad event will happen. Example:

- Well, I have been lucky so far. I haven't had a stroke yet. But who says it couldn't happen any time now?

To challenge, have your client try on the *Rose Colored Glasses* [Sobel and Ornstein (1996)] and do Behavioral Experiments, as follows:

- Are you willing to take the risk of not worrying and see what happens?

- Are you willing to try out the *Rose Colored Glasses,* expect positive things and see what happens? If yes, it involves selectively expecting things to turn out well.

- A *behavioral experiment* involves making a positive prediction about an upcoming worrisome event and later comparing the prediction with what actually took place. (For more information on Behavioral Experiments, see session 5.)

2. **Giving Up**
   This state of mind occurs in a person whose thinking is dominated by the expectation of a negative outcome and no longer wants to exert any effort to change it. Example:

   - I don't know if I have the motivation to go through this treatment. What if I don't want to change my fear of driving? (*When questioned more closely*) Maybe it's too hard or it won't work.

   To challenge, look at past evidence, ask about pros and cons, by asking the following types of questions:

   - Was there ever a time when you felt hopeless about something and it turned around for you? Was there ever joy in your life thereafter?

   - What are the pros and cons of trying?

3. **The Unanswerable Question: Why? Why? Why?**
   Everyone would like to know why something happens, including why he or she developed panic disorder. The best you can do is provide an educated guess based on your knowledge about panic disorder and the client's history and current profile. But some people get "stuck" in this questioning mode, plaguing themselves with a question that cannot be answered definitively. Rather than really trying to find an answer, it becomes a vehicle for self-torture and condemnation. Examples:

   - If I only knew why, I would be fine.

   - Why do I have panic disorder, *why?*

To challenge, help your client switch to a problem-solving mode and/or use "How" or "What" questions. The problem-solving mode is achieved when the client focuses on proactive thinking. The following statement exemplifies this mode:

- I will need to learn all the available skills to overcome my fears. Whatever it takes, however long it takes, I will get there.

Some examples of "How" or "What" questions are:

- What can I do to help decrease my anxiety?
- How can I best learn to cope with panics?

Skill Building

Challenging Automatic Thoughts (Worksheet 4)

This is one of the most important cognitive restructuring methods. You are teaching your client to challenge him or herself, a skill you hope your client will learn for the future as well as now. When fearful, clients tend to revert to their old ways of thinking, e.g., "What's the matter with me? Why can't I do this?" "This is silly. Just do it." "I can do it; I've done it in the past." Such statements, if positive (last example), are simply positive self-statements. They do not bring about change at a deeper level.

Review with your client Worksheet 4: Challenging Automatic Thoughts, 1st Step. Observe if your client identified a specific trigger (in contrast to "I panicked" or "I got anxious") and the exact automatic thought. Note that statements such as "I panicked" are too vague either as a trigger or as an automatic thought. In this context, "panic" is only a vague label that can mean different things to different people. If your client elaborated too much, help him or her find briefer and more concise ways of expressing him or herself. (Make a note of your client's automatic thoughts for later reference.)

Now have your client direct his or her attention to the entire Worksheet 4, including the instructions. The examples provided show how brief the responses should ideally be. This brevity allows the person to stay more focused. (Note, however, that in Example 1 the ensuing embarrassment is the worst part of passing out for that particular person.) Finally, to also aid with the task, make sure your client writes only one automatic thought. Worksheet 4, 1st Step may provide a good illustration. If more than one was written down, were they related and was one clearly the ultimate fear in that same sequence? If more than one automatic thought is generated, e.g., "I will have a stroke or lose control and embarrass myself" (i.e., losing control and feeling embarrassed is separate from the fear of a stroke), then the client should use two worksheets, one for each fear. Or, the client can work with one automatic thought only, targeting the worst of the fears.

Clients need to practice with quite a few samples of the worksheet before it becomes so easy that they can do this in their minds in panic and phobic situations. For this to occur, they need to fill out between seven and ten of these worksheets.

Session Summary

"Today we explored in greater detail the negative automatic thoughts that emerge in panic and phobic situations. I encouraged you to think of them as hypotheses. These hypotheses are often not based on reality but reflect cognitive traps we humans fall into. I went over the five most common irrational thoughts and three most common unhelpful thoughts in panic disorder. Finally, we worked on the entire Worksheet 4."

Feedback from Client

"What questions, aside from what you brought up earlier, do you have about what we reviewed today? Are there any related issues you wish to address?"

Difficulties You May Encounter Identifying Automatic Thoughts

"I have no thoughts, I'm just scared."

This statement, quite a common one, can have various explanations. The client could be very unaware of thoughts, could be resistant to this detailed work, or he or she could feel that this is the only way to portray how terrifying the panic attacks are. Since you do not know in advance what the reason for the statement is, it is safest to assume that your client has a need to hang on to the fearful emotion. Hence, it is often good to take a minute first to validate how fear-provoking the experience must be for the client. Ask your client to describe the "scared" feelings more. If you stay with it and pay attention, most likely your client will express a thought as well. A simple example follows.

Therapist:	So you get really scared when you have panic attacks. That is understandable. Tell me, what are you most scared of?
Client:	I'm just terrified.
Therapist:	I believe I understand your terror. What is the worst part of it?
Client:	I'm just so afraid of doing something stupid.
Therapist:	Like what?
Client:	I could start screaming and making a total fool out of myself.
Therapist:	Has this actually happened?
Client:	No, not yet, but I have been awfully close.
Therapist:	Let me point out to you that what you said about your worst fear, that of screaming and making a total fool of yourself, are precisely the thoughts we are looking for. The reason this is so important is that we now have something very concrete to work on.

Besides direct inquiry, if the client filled out Worksheet 3, which you have been monitoring, then there are bound to be thoughts in it. Also, during the assessment (see Zuercher-White 1997), you might have asked your client what he or she fears in a panic and how likely the feared event could happen. In these cases, you might want to refer to it.

"You are putting thoughts in my mind. They are not necessarily mine."

This can be the response when you have worked with your client to elicit automatic thoughts, particularly when you try to pin down a very specific thought. If this occurs, first validate your client's observation. Then ask your client for permission to pursue this line as one possible hypothesis, primarily for purposes of illustration. You can also say that while you are pursuing this line of reasoning, if a more accurate thought emerges, you can work on the latter. Nonetheless, you might very well be on track with what came up first.

Homework

The homework for session 5 is as follows:

1. Worksheet 1: Panic Frequency and Intensity.

2. Read session 4 in your client manual and bring up any questions or comments.

3. Fill out three samples of Worksheet 4. If you have no panic attack or phobic encounter this week, practice with any experience that produces worry and anxiety. At this time, use *current* panic/phobic/anxious events. Pay attention to the cognitive traps your automatic thoughts represent. (Ask your client again to make copies of the samples of the worksheet for you to review and for future reference. You are not likely to review all samples in the session and may wish to look at them in between the sessions for subsequent feedback.)

If agoraphobia is present:

4. Exposures (for the client to record on Worksheet 10 and you on Therapist Record 10T, under "Planned Exposures"). This homework was probably set in the beginning of the session.

Worksheet 4: Challenging Automatic Thoughts

1. Date.

_____

2. Specific Trigger: **Situation and/or physical symptom.**

_____

3. Automatic Thought (Negative Thought). **The *exact* bad thing that will happen if you feel or do** (write #2 here): _____
   is:

   How strongly do you believe your Automatic Thought will happen, 0–100%? _____

4. My Evidence. **Why do you think #3, your Automatic Thought, will happen?**

   Then Refute!

_____

5. Alternative Thought(s) (Positive Thought). **Can the trigger (#2 above) have an explanation/lead to something** (other than #3) **with a harmless result?** List 1–3 with the probability of each, from 0–100%.

_____

6. Face Up to Automatic Thought (#3). **"Just because** _____ **does not mean** _____**"** or **"So what if** _____**!"**

   How strongly do you believe in your Automatic Thought (#3) NOW, 0–100%? _____

Instructions to Worksheet 4: Challenging Automatic Thoughts

1. Date. By always recording the date, you will be able to monitor your progress over time.

2. Specific Trigger: **Situation** (driving over the bridge, going to the mall) **and/or physical symptom** (dizziness, tightness in chest, numbness in arms). What brought on your fear thought (Automatic Thought)? (Don't write "panic" or "anxiety," but what *specifically* in the panic or anxiety made you afraid.)

3. Automatic Thought (Negative Thought). **The *exact* bad thing that will happen if you feel or do** (write #2 here): _____
   is: The thought should be stated in the form of a *specific theory/prediction* (not as a question, e.g., "I will have a heart attack and die," not "Will I have a heart attack and die?").
   Questions to guide you: What are you afraid might happen with these symptoms? What's the worst thing that you think will happen in this situation?

   How strongly do you believe your Automatic Thought will happen, 0–100%? _____

4. My Evidence. **Why do you think #3, your Automatic Thought, will happen?** It is the evidence (proof) used for your Automatic Thought.

   Then Refute! You can refute your evidence based on past experience, logic, and other evidence (e.g., do your emotions really dictate your behavior?).

5. Alternative Thought(s) (Positive Thought). **Can the trigger (#2 above) have an explanation/lead to something** (other than #3) **with a harmless result?** List 1–3 with probability of each, 0–100%.
   Questions to guide you: Are you falling into a cognitive trap? What else makes these sensations happen? Does it really matter what others think?

6. Face Up to Automatic Thought (#3). **"Just because (#2) occurs, does not mean (#3) will too,"** or **"So what if (#2) happens!** It's not the end of the world!" (Apply "So what if _____ " to social fears.)

   How strongly do you believe in your Automatic Thought (#3) NOW, 0–100%? _____

Worksheet 4: Challenging Automatic Thoughts

1. Date. 7-28-99

2. Specific Trigger: **Situation and/or physical symptom**.
   I was shopping in the grocery store. I felt fearful and felt tightness in my throat.

3. Automatic Thought (Negative Thought). **The *exact* bad thing that will happen if you feel or do** (write #2 here): *Feeling tightness in my throat*
   is: *Pass out from lack of air and feel totally embarrassed.*

   How strongly do you believe your Automatic Thought will happen, 0–100%? _60%_

4. My Evidence. **Why do you think #3, your Automatic Thought, will happen?**
   If I pass out, I'll feel totally self-conscious. Other people don't faint because of anxiety.

   Then Refute!
   I've had it happen before and I've gotten through it without fainting.

5. Alternative Thought(s) (Positive Thought). **Can the trigger (#2 above) have an explanation/lead to something** (other than #3) **with a harmless result?** List 1–3 with probability of each, 0–100%.
   * *First of all, I'm breathing all along; I'm probably overbreathing rather than not breathing. 80%.*
   * *I need to stay and the anxiety will decrease. 70%.*
   * *Even if I were to faint, no one would know why, and people would probably be concerned. 90%.*

6. Face Up to Automatic Thought (#3). **"Just because _____ occurs, does not mean _____ will too."** or **"So what if _____ happens!"**
   Just because I feel tightness in my throat does not mean I'll faint. And if I fainted and felt embarrassed, so what! It's not the end of the world.

   How strongly do you believe in your Automatic Thought (#3) NOW, 0–100%? _30%_

Example 2: Challenging Automatic Thoughts

Worksheet 4: Challenging Automatic Thoughts

1. Date. 9-7-99

2. Specific Trigger: **Situation and/or physical symptom.**
   I was at a restaurant where in the past I've had high anxiety and feelings of unreality.

3. Automatic Thought (Negative Thought). **The *exact* bad thing that will happen if you feel or do** (write #2 here): *Feelings of unreality*
   is: *I can't be relaxed and enjoy myself like everyone else around me. If I let my guard down, I'll lose control and will end up with a permanently foggy state of mind.*

   How strongly do you believe your Automatic Thought will happen, 0–100%? 80%

4. My Evidence. **Why do you think #3, your Automatic Thought, will happen?**
   These feelings of unreality are not normal. They are signs of a nervous breakdown.

   Then Refute!
   I've felt this way before and have not had a nervous breakdown.

5. Alternative Thought(s) (Positive Thought). **Can the trigger (#2 above) have an explanation/lead to something** (other than #3) **with a harmless result?** List 1–3 with probability of each, 0–100%.
   * *I might have been overbreathing. 50%.*
   * *I cannot control all my feelings. I can allow these feelings of unreality to float through me. 80%.*

6. Face Up to Automatic Thought (#3). **"Just because _____ occurs, does not mean _____ will too."** or **"So what if _____ happens!"**
   Just because I have had these feelings in the restaurant, does not mean I'll always feel anxious and unreal. And if I felt that, they are not signs of a nervous breakdown.

   How strongly do you believe in your Automatic Thought (#3) NOW, 0–100%? 30%

Session 5

Cognitive Restructuring: Addressing the Focal Fears, Further Methods to Challenge Fears

---

Monitoring of Current Status

Review Worksheet 1: Panic Frequency and Intensity. Proceed as in session 1.

Agenda

Review in advance of this session the fears your client stated having in a panic in the assessment session, thoughts written down on Worksheet 3, and the automatic thoughts that your client worked with on Worksheet 4, 1st Step. You want to concentrate now on your client's *worst* fear—the so-called *focal fear*. When you review the samples of Worksheet 4: Challenging Automatic Thoughts, which your client brought in, compare these fears to the information you reviewed prior to the session to assess if a focal fear was addressed.

After reviewing the current samples of Worksheet 4, you can point to the focal fear/s, if not already done so. If not yet addressed, use the most recent panic attack (or phobic encounter) or another "bad" panic attack. For instance, in an attempt to capture the focal fear have your client describe the worst panic attack he or she has had.

After reviewing any one of the worksheets, ask your client which cognitive trap his or her automatic thought represents. If relevant, challenge the client in his or her use of this particular cognitive trap (see session 4). You will also have other tools from this chapter at hand to challenge your client's fears. (For a more complete list of methods, consult *Treating Panic Disorder and Agoraphobia: A Step-by-Step Clinical Guide*, Zuercher-White 1997.)

Review of Homework

The homework assignments that you are following up since session 4 are:

1. Worksheet 1: Panic Frequency and Intensity.

2. Reading session 4 in the client manual.

3. Three samples of Worksheet 4: Challenging Automatic Thoughts. (Ask to see all three samples, but you may have time to review only one closely, especially if your client needs help in perfecting it.)

If agoraphobia is present:

4. Exposures as recorded on Worksheet 10: Your Weekly Exposures, under "Actual Effort." Plan new exposures with your client.

Concepts and Skills

The focal fear is the worst fear the client has. There is usually one worst fear, sometimes two or even three. A number of more superficial fears are related to the focal fear. For instance, in Example 1 of Worksheet 4: Challenging Automatic Thoughts (see session 4), embarrassment is the focal fear, while for another client fainting *per se* may be the focal fear. One way to help clarify is to ask your client in the former case if he or she would be fearful of fainting if strangers were not around. If the person says no, then it is rather obvious that he or she fears the social repercussions. On the other hand, if the client is very fearful of fainting anywhere, then this is also a focal fear. You must address the worst fears for your client to improve. The most typical focal fears are described in the sections that follow.

Psychoeducation

When you educate your client about his or her focal fears, do not simply lecture. Instead, weave this information into the challenges you pose to your client. Use a Socratic dialogue as much as possible.

Working On and Challenging Focal Fears

The Focal Fear of Dying from a Heart Attack: Feared symptoms in a panic are usually palpitations, heart racing, heart fluttering, skipped heartbeats, and chest pain.

Medical fact: Panic attacks do not lead to heart attacks. On an electrocardiogram test (EKG), a panic attack shows up as just a slightly increased heart rate. Your client can ask his or her physician about what the actual symptoms of a heart attack are. These usually involve very strong pressure in the chest, intense chest pain, and only occasionally, palpitations. The symptoms often diminish with rest. In contrast, when the anxious or panicked person lies down, the symptoms frequently persist.

The Focal Fear of Dying from Suffocation: Fears of suffocation seem to be on the increase. The feared symptoms are usually the sensation of not getting enough air, i.e., breathlessness, the throat closing up, choking sensations, or chest pressure. Just being in an enclosed, hot, and/or crowded place often causes the client to believe that he or she will not get enough air.

Medical fact: People do not die from suffocation during a panic. Although it is extremely common for people to *feel* as if they were not breathing, they actually are breathing all along. In fact, the harder they try to breathe, the more likely it is that they might hyperventilate. The perception is paradoxical, because when hyperventilating, the person breathes in too much air, all the while having the sensation of not getting enough air.

The Focal Fear of Having a Stroke: Symptoms interpreted by clients as those leading to a stroke are numbness, stiffness, tingling, sensations of weakness (especially if perceived on one side of the body), and/or a heat wave moving up the spine to the head. This fear develops often if there is a history of strokes in the client's family.

Medical fact: Panic attacks do not lead to strokes. When blood pressure rises during a panic attack, it does so only slightly, not enough to trigger a stroke.

The Focal Fear of Fainting: Sensations leading to this fear are light-headedness, dizziness, feelings of faintness, numbness, blurred or tunnel vision, inability to concentrate, feeling hot, and being unable to breathe. This fear goes hand in hand with the fear of collapse. Often, when the client says that he or she is afraid of collapsing, fear of fainting is behind the fear of collapse. Hence, always ask your client what is meant by "collapse." If your client claims to have fainted, ask for a detailed account. Many clients use the term "fainting" to indicate feeling very close to fainting. This is a very different physiological state than lying on the ground unconscious, even if only for a few seconds.

Medical fact: People do not faint from panics, except in very rare circumstances. This is because blood pressure rises slightly during the physiological arousal in panic. For someone to faint, the blood pressure must plummet, involving the parasympathetic nervous system. Fading away is the most typical sensation prior to actual fainting. (People with blood-injection-injury phobias constitute the exception; they sometimes do faint. There is a sudden drop in their blood pressure.)

The Focal Fear of Going Crazy or Having a Nervous Breakdown: The feared symptoms are often feelings of unreality or depersonalization, losing the ability to focus and concentrate, racing thoughts, feeling dominated by fear with the belief that the fear will damage the person's nerves forever, unusual thoughts and bizarre images, and the mind going blank. When these clients feel that they cannot "control" their thinking, they interpret that as a sign of beginning madness.

Medical fact: Panic attacks do not lead to insanity. A schizophrenic may have panic attacks in addition to the psychosis, but panic disorder does not lead to schizophrenia. If someone does have a "nervous breakdown," it is never solely due to panic disorder. There are probably a *number* of other psychological and maybe physiological factors involved. It is normal at times for people to have strange, bizarre thoughts and images. It is also common for people to feel so stressed at times that it is hard to cope, concentrate, and focus.

The Focal Fear of Losing Control: "Losing control" tends to be an emotionally loaded expression, often involving catastrophizing errors. The term is vague, and it needs to be broken down into the *specific* fear involved. For instance, the strong impulse to run during the fight/flight response is thought of by many people as losing control. Others fear crying, running and screaming, becoming paralyzed with fear, frightening others, having a sensation described as "crawling out of their skin," etc.

Medical fact: The fight/flight response actually *increases* the ability to think faster and more clearly. However, the thoughts are focused on the threat. Some people label crying as losing control. Here, it is helpful to show the person how to accept crying as a normal human emotion, even though there are situations where they might prefer not to cry.

The Focal Fear of Being Embarrassed or Humiliated: The fears here are closely associated with those of losing control. Feared symptoms are shaking, trembling, crying, blushing, unsteady or cracking voice. There is a common fear of being thought of as "anxious," as if anxiety were a crime. Many clients view anxiety as weakness, which they disdain. Some of my clients fear running, leaving a meeting, a queue, a store, or collapsing. They are mostly afraid that others will think of them as "crazy," "weird," or "strange."

Medical fact: It is a reality for everyone to sometimes do or say something that feels embarrassing or humiliating. Although no one looks forward to it, we all can learn to survive it.

The Focal Fear of Feeling so Weak That One Cannot Move or Will Fall Down: The feared sensations are numbness, tingling, extreme weakness, feeling "wobbly." The weakness is felt especially in the knees and legs, sometimes in the arms. Some people feel extreme stiffness and heaviness.

Medical fact: Even when people feel weak, numb, and stiff when anxious, that does not mean that their muscles are too weak to support them. It is a *perception,* and the person assumes that it is not possible to move, stand, or drive under those circumstances.

Skill Building

Belief Ratings

Belief ratings are a measure of how strongly a thought is believed. You can use them to challenge your client's fears and also to assess progress during treatment. Have your client rate the belief in the feared disaster on a 0–100 percent scale.

0 percent = The fearful thought is not believed at all.
50 percent = The thought is believed halfway.
100 percent = The person is totally convinced that the thought is true.

Challenging the Belief Rating: Putting It to a Logical Test: The belief rating is used in two time frames: While sitting here right *now,* and *then,* i.e., in the middle of a bad panic attack.

Example:

Therapist:	Sitting here right now, using the scale from 0 to 100, how strongly do you believe that the difficulty you have breathing in a panic will lead you to suffocate?
Client:	Oh, I know it won't happen; maybe 30 percent.
Therapist:	If you were totally convinced it won't happen, you wouldn't have the thought and the fear, isn't that true? So you think about 30 percent. And in the middle of a panic, when you feel the same sensations, how strongly do you believe it then?
Client:	About 85 percent. (Clients often will give you a higher rating for the thought during the panic.)
Therapist:	Can you tell me how the probability changes during the panic compared with now?
Client:	Right now I'm not scared.
Therapist:	You are right. When a person feels anxious, they have anxious thoughts. This is what happens to you. Now, let's look at this more closely. Let's use an analogy. You don't have diabetes, do you?
Client:	No.
Therapist:	Good. If you happened to see a program on TV, let's say, on how bad diabetes can be, and you got scared for a moment thinking how awful it would be to live with diabetes, would it increase your probability of contracting the disease compared to if you never thought of it? In other words, my question is whether you think the probability changes just based on your thought.
Client:	No, I guess it won't change the probability.
Therapist:	Do you think it may apply here? That is, how does the probability change, based on your thought?
Client:	I don't know, but I fear it could happen.
Therapist:	If it *could* happen some day that the sensation of suffocation really led you to die, what would be a more accurate probability?
Client:	Oh, maybe 5 percent.
Therapist:	Okay. Your next challenge is to see if you can think this way the next time you have a panic and it seems difficult to breathe. You can use Worksheet 4: Challenging Automatic Thoughts to aid you in this challenge. Remember, you need to practice with the worksheet enough so that you can do it later quickly in your head. You need to look for the evidence, then refute it, look for alternative hypotheses. Finally, face up to the thought that you will suffocate to death.

(Now you might pursue this line of questioning, having your client tell you the evidence, how to refute it, alternative thoughts, etc.)

Assessing Treatment Progress with Belief Ratings: The belief ratings can be used within sessions as well as across sessions. Is the cognitive restructuring having an impact? You can pursue the same fear over time and see what is happening with the belief rating. You are also teaching your client to take responsibility for his or her fearful thoughts. In other words, it is easy for a client to throw out a number, but it is very different to have to defend it.

Behavioral Experiments (The Experimental Method)

This involves putting the idea to a behavioral test. It is another way of questioning the credibility of the fearful automatic thought. A powerful behavioral test may often provide stronger evidence that the automatic thought is erroneous than a purely verbal challenge. However, it is not always possible to put the thought to a behavioral test. Also, verbal challenges are good compliments to the behavioral ones.

Doing Without Safety Signals and Safety Behaviors: Effective behavioral experiments involve eliminating the client's use of safety signals and safety behaviors. Common safety signals are going to places accompanied, carrying medications, water, a paper bag to breathe into, a telephone, phone numbers of hospitals, etc. Common safety behaviors are white-knuckling while driving, sitting down, and holding on to a shopping cart (when feeling faint); making a strong effort to control one's thoughts (to prevent insanity). When clients tell you that they do many exposures and yet continue to feel fear, they are very likely using safety signals or safety behaviors. These experiments can be started initially with small steps. Afterwards, ask your client why a feared catastrophic outcome did not occur.

Empirical Hypothesis Testing: Behavioral experiments should be set up so as to maximize a positive outcome. If properly planned, they can be powerful agents of cognitive change. You and your client together can set up experiments that are expected to yield the desired evidence. Your client's input is crucial to know precisely how his or her fear can be disconfirmed. Afterwards, always compare the prediction with the actual outcome and have your client draw a conclusion based on this.

Example of a behavioral experiment:

Therapist: You say that when you panic while driving, you fear the anxiety could prevent you from keeping the wheel in the right place and you may veer across to another lane. Is this correct?

Client: Yes.

Therapist: Let's see if we can translate this into a behavioral experiment. How often does it happen that you panic or at least get very anxious while driving on major thoroughfares? Can you give me a percentage?

Client: About 75 percent of the time.

Therapist: Let me propose an experiment to you and let me know if this is reasonable for you to carry out. The aim of the experiment is to test out whether you will lose control of the car when you get very anxious or have a full panic. Plan on one to three driving exposures this week, using major thoroughfares. Since this is your first experiment, choose times and places where there is very little traffic, even if it means driving at five A.M. or six A.M. on Saturday and Sunday. At least one of the times you are bound to get very anxious, if not have a panic attack. Your task is to keep driving in spite of anxiety and panic, if at all possible. See what happens, whether you cross the white lines inappropriately or not. You will obviously need to keep focused on the here-and-now. What do you think? Does this sound reasonable?

Client: Yes.

Therapist: Okay, one more thing. What would it mean if you did not veer off course inappropriately?

Client: I guess that I can still function in spite of anxiety and panic.

Therapist: You guess, or are you pretty sure it would show you can still drive safely?

Client: It would show I could drive safely.

Therapist: Great! I'll pursue this when we meet the next time.

In the next session:

Therapist: How did your driving go?

Client: Well.

Therapist: Did you get anxious?

Client: Yes, I got very anxious, but I had no panic.

Therapist: Good enough. So you did not veer off course?

Client: No.

Therapist: Was this consistent with your initial theory?

Client: No.

Therapist: What conclusion can you draw from this experiment?

Client: I'm in control more than I think I am. But I am still not sure if I have a full-blown panic.

Therapist: Your conclusion is still very good. This was only the first step. Now, the next time you have a panic while driving, if at all possible try to continue driving and see what happens. Please let me know if you have one and how you do.

Session Summary

"We reviewed your samples of Worksheet 4. As you saw, it is crucial to do it well and in as brief format as possible. We identified your focal fears. You have started to work on them, but you need to fill out more samples of Worksheet 4 as pertaining to your focal fears. Remember that the easier it is to do it in writing, the more likely it will be that you will learn to do it in your head. This is one of the most crucial skills you can learn to combat your panic disorder.

"You are now learning to increasingly take responsibility for your automatic thoughts. For your recovery, you must be aware of what happens to your thoughts when you feel scared. Observe what happens to the probability of those automatic thoughts when you are in the process of challenging them and also over time, across different samples of Worksheet 4. Finally, we planned a behavioral experiment for you to test out in real life what happens with your assumption. Does the assumption hold water?"

Feedback from Client

"What questions, aside from what you brought up earlier, do you have about what we reviewed today? Are there any related issues you wish to address?"

Difficulties You May Encounter

Your Client Filled Out None or One Sample of Worksheet 4

Here, you may first listen to what your client says. What are the reasons? If no time, it may have to do with motivation. Other possibilities are that the worksheet requires too much effort. If there are any difficulties filling it out, you can go over with your client a previous one in detail and review strengths and weaknesses in the sample. It is also possible that your client thinks that the first few were enough, and is running out of steam, so to speak. In contrast, the worksheet is more useful the more it is repeated. Clients who persevere and fill out six to ten of the full worksheet say invariably that they find it very helpful. Although the purpose of the worksheet is to weaken the original automatic thought and replace it with alternative thoughts, a number of clients find it to be a reassuring tool. It helps them shift from being caught in catastrophic fear to a more flexible mode by following a very concrete level of reasoning.

Homework

The homework for session 6 is as follows:

1. Worksheet 1: Panic Frequency and Intensity.

2. Read session 5 in your book and bring up any questions or comments.

3. Fill out three samples of Worksheet 4. If you have no panic attack or phobic encounter this week, practice with any experience that produces worry and anxiety. However, it is especially useful if you confront your focal fear. Pay attention to the cognitive traps your automatic thoughts represent. (Ask your client again, if possible, to make you copies of the samples of the worksheet for future reference.)

If agoraphobia is present:

4. Exposures (for the client to record on Worksheet 10 and you on Therapist Record 10T, under "Planned Exposures"). This homework was probably set in the beginning of the session.

Session 6

Cognitive Restructuring: Continuing to Challenge Fears, Changing Core Beliefs

Monitoring of Current Status

Review Worksheet 1: Panic Frequency and Intensity. Proceed as in session 1.

Agenda

Evaluate your client's progress with his or her automatic thoughts. Has your client filled out at least six samples of Worksheet 4? In addition, how strong is your client's belief in the validity of the automatic thoughts? If the fear has not decreased significantly, you may need to stay with the task using the techniques you already have. You will in either case continue to do cognitive restructuring throughout the end of the treatment. For instance, you will be able to combine it well with any fears that emerge in the interoceptive exposure work, sessions 7 through 9.

If your client has progressed well so far and if there is interest, you may wish to work with your client's core beliefs. Also, if your client's fears persist strongly in spite of a good effort with Worksheet 4, it is possible that core belief work is indicated. However, remember that core belief work is not required in the treatment of panic disorder.

Review of Homework

The homework assignments that you are following up since session 5 are:

1. Worksheet 1: Panic Frequency and Intensity.

2. Reading session 5 in the client manual.

3. Three samples of Worksheet 4: Challenging Automatic Thoughts, preferably pertaining to focal fears. Ask your client which cognitive trap his or her automatic thought represents.

If agoraphobia is present:

4. Exposures as recorded on Worksheet 10: Your Weekly Exposures, under "Actual Effort." Plan new exposures with your client.

Concepts and Skills

If your client's fear of panic symptoms has not diminished sufficiently, you may wish to continue working on the automatic thoughts. You can do so via Worksheet 4 and/or use any of the other techniques to challenge your client's fears.

Sometimes your client does not seem to progress because in fact there may be core beliefs maintaining the automatic thoughts. Core beliefs are basic beliefs we hold about ourselves, others, and about life and the world. We will work primarily with core beliefs pertaining to the self. Core beliefs must be identified before they can be changed. (The reader is referred to Beck 1995; Burns 1989; and Greenberger and Padesky 1995.)

Once you have identified a core belief, you can use an evidence continuum to determine where the client stands in regards to the continuum in comparison with other people. With your help, your client needs to choose an appropriate new core belief, which he or she wishes to live by. Finally, you teach your client how to work on the core belief log. This work must be monitored then throughout the end of treatment, parallel with the other work you will be doing. (It takes only a few minutes to ask what has been entered in the log.)

Psychoeducation

Identifying Assumptions and Core Beliefs

Core beliefs can often be accessed via automatic thoughts and assumptions. They can also be identified through the process of unfolding the belief.

Ask Your Client Directly About His or Her Core Belief: Your client's automatic thoughts may already have revealed a possible core belief. In this case, you can ask your client directly about it.

Example:

Client: When I have a panic, I feel detached, totally black, empty; I have a bad feeling about myself.

Therapist:	Is there something bad about you? Could your negative core belief be that you are bad?
Client:	No, that does not feel right. It's just feeling totally black, detached. That's when I have on occasion thoughts of suicide. (This has already been checked out. The client is not actively suicidal.)
Therapist:	Let me venture to say that you have a core belief that says, "I'm detached." Does it sound like it fits?
Client:	Yes. (The client then elaborated on how she had felt detached since childhood and into her present life.)

Look for Common Themes Across the Automatic Thoughts: Observe what automatic thoughts and other expressions the person uses. Sometimes themes are repeated, giving a good clue as to the core belief.
> Example:

Therapist:	Esther, do you see a common word or image running through your automatic thoughts?
Client:	Well, it is true that in almost all my worksheets I put down the word crazy. It's true; the fear is so much there, not just when I have panic attacks.

Sentence Completion Method: The types of sentences used here are (Padesky 1994): "I am _____," "Other people are _____," "Life is _____." Look for a brief answer, preferably stated in one word.
> Example:

Therapist:	You want to always be in control. What's the thought behind this? *Not having control of myself at all times would mean . . .*
Client:	I don't have my own identity.

Let Assumptions Lead You to Core Beliefs: Since assumptions are closely linked to core beliefs they can sometimes lead the way to them. One way is to help the client change "should" to "If . . . it means" statements.
> Example 1:

Client:	I shouldn't fail in this new job.
Therapist:	Can you change it to an "If . . . it means" statement? *If I fail in this job, it means* (what it says about you) _____.
Client:	If I fail in this job, it means I'll be defeated again.

The likely core belief is, "I'm defeated."

> Example 2:

Client:	I should be able to control my anxiety like everyone else.
Therapist:	Can you change it to an "If . . . it means" statement? *If I can't control my anxiety, it means* (what it says about you) _____.
Client:	If I can't control my anxiety, it means I'll never be sure of myself.

The core belief could be, "I'm insecure."

Unfolding the Belief: Unfolding the belief is what Burns (1989) describes as the "vertical arrow or the top down technique." This technique involves asking a series of questions, which should lead to deeper levels of thought, and hopefully to the underlying core belief. You go as far as you can. When arriving at a core belief, there is often a shift in affect (often deep sadness) when the client expresses a very basic belief about him or herself. If you do not seem to arrive at a basic belief and the same thought is repeated in the same or similar words, you may have come to an impasse. Other times it could mean that there is a positive or a somewhat negative but flexible belief (e.g., the belief may be in the process of change). Worksheet 5: Unfolding the Belief illustrates the process, using the questions and statements provided below. The worksheet, followed by an example, can be found at the end of this session.

Questions and Statements to Unfold the Belief

1. State the belief as a theory.

2. Be as *specific* as possible.

3. If _____ happened, *why* would it be so upsetting to you?

4. If this thought were true, what would it mean to you?

5. What does that say about you?

6. Why would that be upsetting?

7. And what would that *mean* to you?

8. What's the *worst* thing that could happen?

9. And then what?

At the very end of the unfolding process, if you have arrived at a possible reason for the belief, you can remark:

10. So *because* _____, you *believe* _____.

And follow that up with:

11. How long have you held that belief?

Skill Building

Changing Core Beliefs

Once you have identified a negative core belief, ask your client why he or she would want to change it. Your client is likely to give some good examples of how it has produced distress. The next step is to identify a corresponding modified or new core belief. (Padesky, 1994, suggests that a new belief be identified as soon as possible.) Ask your client which new rule he or she would like to live by. "If you did not live by the belief _____ (old core belief), which alternative belief would you feel more comfortable with? One that would make you feel really good about yourself?" The alternative new belief should seldom be stated as the exact opposite. For example, a client's original core belief was, "Conceit brings punishment." The repercussions of this belief was that the client never allowed himself to feel totally good or joyful, let alone happy. When good feelings came on, they would immediately be followed by a cloud. The alternative belief to strive for would not be "Conceit is good." This client chose as a new core belief simply, "It's good to feel great."

There are two ways of working on changing core beliefs, using an evidence continuum and a core belief log (Padesky 1994). These methods are simpler to use than challenging automatic thoughts, but they require tenacity over a longer period of time—six to twelve months according to Padesky.

Evidence Continuum: Work with evidence continua should be done in writing, preferably with a blackboard. This allows you and your client to conceptualize the task and absorb its meaning. Padesky suggests that continua be done specifically with the new, positive belief instead of the old core belief. That is, have your client put energy into working on strengthening the new belief, not the old one. When you work with your client, draw a horizontal line on the blackboard, an Evidence Continuum, and write the extreme positions at the ends, 0 percent to 100 percent. The end points must reflect extreme points if it is to work. Other points of the continuum can also be numbered with 25 percent, 50 percent, and 75 percent.

Example:

The client's old core belief was "I'm fragile." She identified as the new core belief to live by, "Most of the time I'm able to cope."

New core belief: Most of the time I'm able to cope.

0%
Never able to cope

Coping Continuum

100%
Always able to cope

Now ask your client for the names of a few people he or she knows, some of whom he or she likes and admires and others not. Now have your client place these people on the coping continuum. Last, have the person place himself or herself there. People usually do not rate themselves at 0 in these scales. The aim is to show that people have different degrees of coping ability, and that it is not the only quality that makes them likeable or unlikeable.

Criteria Continua: According to Padesky (1994), people's negative beliefs are often global and judgmental. The picture changes when the beliefs are translated into specific behavioral criteria. To illustrate, the client in the above example, when asked what constitutes "coping ability," said: "Looking for solutions when confronted with problems," "Standing up again if you fall," "Keeping a hopeful attitude," "Finding a new path if the old one is blocked." A new criteria continuum from 0 to 100 is now drawn up for each of the stated attributes. Again, as with the evidence continuum, the end points must reflect extremes for it to work. The client is asked to rate the others and himself or herself along these criteria continua, just as was done with the original evidence continuum. Clients usually rate themselves higher along these criteria than along the original evidence continuum. Ask your client what he or she observes from the contrast; this can be quite revealing to the client.

The task is now for the client to evaluate at regular invervals, usually weekly, where along this new core belief continuum he or she falls. This will help increase awareness and preferably lead to increased movement toward the new core belief.

Core Belief Log: Worksheet 6: Core Belief Log allows the client to organize his or her thinking about the new core belief and to start working on it. Having simply identified the old core belief and choosing an alternative will *not* bring about change. The process of believing in a new, modified belief often takes from six to twelve months, as mentioned previously. I have found that about half the clients are willing to work on this worksheet in a consistent manner. They benefit greatly, and they often take pleasure in the process of listing the relevant experiences. Some clients struggle greatly initially and need encouragement until they are comfortable with it.

This log will help the client gather relevant information. Experiences that prove the old core belief are not noted. When an experience occurs that reinforces the old core belief, instruct your client to see what he or she can learn from it and go on. Instead, experiences that reinforce the new core belief are the ones listed. The worksheet, followed by an example, can be found at the end of this session. (After having started to list the experiences supporting the new core belief, future worksheets should essentially start from item #3.)

Summary of Session

"You have made progress with your automatic thoughts. Remember that the fear of the symptoms must diminish for your to overcome panic disorder. You will continue to work with Worksheet 4, but you want to start to challenge your thoughts this way increasingly in your mind.

"We have identified an old core belief that makes you feel badly about yourself. We labeled a new core belief that you want to live by. In this vain, we explored where you stand on an Evidence Continuum and went over Worksheet 6: Core Belief Log."

Feedback from Client

"What questions, aside from what you brought up earlier, do you have about what we reviewed today? Are there any related issues you wish to address?"

Difficulties You May Encounter

You Cannot Identify a Core Belief in Your Client

Sometimes it is difficult to identify relevant core beliefs. The core belief you came up with did not seem to fit or was not relevant. Indeed, your client must feel that the core belief "fits," and you must get a sense that this is workable. One of my clients had a fear of driving over forty miles an hour. Since her general cautiousness was pervasive, we identified the core belief "I must avoid physical harm at all costs." While it was not feasible for her to change this basic way of looking at life, repeated *in vivo* exposure helped increase her driving speed.

Your Client Does Not Record Entries in the Core Belief Log

(If at all, this is likely to come up in session 7.)

Although most clients are very interested in identifying negative core beliefs and choosing positive alternatives, not everyone will end up working on it. I do not usually push the issue. Instead, I give ample praise if they do.

Therapist: You have not made any entries in your Core Belief Log. Was there a particular reason?

Client: I don't know; I couldn't think of anything to record.

Therapist: Let's look at this. Your new core belief is: "I am strong much of the time." Did anything happen this week to support it?

Client: Not really.

Therapist: You did not do anything this week that showed your strength?

Client: No.

Therapist: This may be so. But it is often very hard to actually start seeing yourself in a different light. Tell me briefly what your week was like.

The client tells of a project he worked on, which involved preparing to bid for a contract.

Therapist: Did you feel good about how you prepared for it?

Client: Yes, because I really researched the issue, and I'm as prepared as I can be.

Therapist: Great! I think this qualifies for your Core Belief Log. I bet you take many things that reveal your strength for granted. How about trying this week again? And remember, it does not have to be a big step like this one to deserve being recorded in the log.

Homework

The homework for session 7 is as follows:

1. Worksheet 1: Panic Frequency and Intensity

2. Panic Attack Cognitions Questionnaire and, if agoraphobia is present, Self-Efficacy Scales for Agoraphobia.

3. Read session 6 in the client manual and bring up any questions or comments.

4. Continue to fill out samples of Worksheet 4, as needed.

5. Fill out Worksheet 5, if relevant. Start to make entries in Worksheet 6. "Furthermore, I would like you to give me weekly the percentage that shows where you think you stand on the continuum of your new core belief. Could I leave this up to you to report? With all the other homework, I may forget to ask you this one."

If agoraphobia is present:

6. Exposures (for the client to record on Worksheet 10 and you on Therapist Record 10T, under "Planned Exposures"). This homework was probably set in the beginning of the session.

Worksheet 5: Unfolding the Belief

Automatic Thought	Unfolding the Belief (top down)

Example: Unfolding the Belief

Worksheet 5: Unfolding the Belief

Automatic Thought	Unfolding the Belief (top down)
I started to make a list of what I needed to do, and then I panicked.	
	What exactly scared you?
It reminded me of this anxiety. The anxiety will last forever. (This is the automatic thought.)	
	If that happened, why would it be so upsetting to you?
When I keep getting anxious, I'm losing more control over my life.	
	What would that mean to you?
I'll wander endlessly without aim.	
	If that were true, what would it mean to you?
I might become a crazy maniac and not cope with the world.	
	If that were true, what would it say about you?
I should never have been born.	
	Why would you come to this conclusion?
I'm too fragile for this world.	
	So, ongoing anxiety shows you are too fragile for this world. Is that true?
Yes.	
	How long have you held the belief that you are too fragile for this world?
When I was small, I was quite ill and consequently overprotected. Others always rescued me. I felt I was too fragile.	

Worksheet 6: Core Belief Log

1. Old Core Belief.

_____

2. Why I want to change my old Core Belief.

_____

3. New Core Belief (state a Core Belief that is more user-friendly).

_____

4. List current and future experiences (however small) that support the New Core Belief.

Date	Experiences

This list is to be continued for a number of months to really effect change.

Worksheet 6: Core Belief Log

1. Old Core Belief.   *I'm fragile.*

2. Why I want to change my old Core Belief.
   I feel weak, unable to cope. The panic attacks just help prove to me how badly I cope.

3. New Core Belief (State a Core Belief that is more user-friendly.)
   Most of the time I'm able to cope.

4. List current and future experiences (however small) that support the New Core Belief.

Date	Experiences
6-30-99	*I had a panic attack while standing in a long line in the bank. This time I did not escape.*
7-2-99	*My boss tried to push me to work faster on a big project. I stood up to him and explained how I was doing my best. (In the past I would have been silent and tried to rush more.)*
7-8-99	*I woke up feeling anxious; it usually signals a "bad" day. This time I got up quickly and got busy, deciding to ignore it. The fear surely tried to creep up on me, but later I forgot about it.*
	(And so forth.)

Interoceptive Exposure: Identifying Fear-Provoking Exercises

Monitoring of Current Status

Review Worksheet 1: Panic Frequency and Intensity, the Panic Attack Cognitions Questionnaire, and, if agoraphobia is present, Self-Efficacy Scales for Agoraphobia. Proceed as in session 1.

Agenda

In this segment of the treatment, you are going to use a behavioral approach to help your client confront feared sensations. Explain to your client the reason behind this important work. After going over the exclusionary criteria and the instructions, cover the basic list of exercises and have your client rate how fearful he or she felt. This will eventually be combined with the cognitive techniques used previously.

Review of Homework

The homework assignments that you are following up since session 6 are:

1. Worksheet 1: Panic Frequency and Intensity.

2. Panic Attack Cognitions Questionnaire and, if agoraphobia is present, Self-Efficacy Scales for Agoraphobia.

3. Reading session 6 in the client manual.

4. Possible samples of Worksheet 4, as needed.

5. Worksheet 5, if relevant. Entries in Worksheet 6. The percentage showing where the client stands on the continuum of the new core belief.

If agoraphobia is present:

6. Exposures as recorded on Worksheet 10, "Actual Effort." Plan new exposures with your client.

Concepts and Skills

Barlow (1986, 1988) and Argyle (1988) emphasize another aspect of fear acquisition: conditioning. Fear has been shown to condition easily to internal, "interoceptive" cues (stimuli arising from the body), just as there can be a conditioned association between fear and phobic situations. Most of the interoceptive exercises were initially listed by Barlow and Craske in the 1989 version of their *Mastery of Your Anxiety and Panic* (see the new edition, MAP II, 1994; see also *Therapist's Guide for the Mastery of Your Anxiety and Panic II* and *Agoraphobia Supplement*, Craske, Meadows, and Barlow 1994). Barlow and Craske were instrumental in the development of the list of exercises listed here. These and other exercises are used by many clinicians.

In this session you and your client will go through the list of the twelve exercises in table 7.1. The aim is to find at least a few exercises that elicit sensations producing fear, expressed in SUDS. These are recorded in Worksheet 7: Interoceptive Exposure Record, a copy of which you should provide to the client. At the end of the session, you will collect the worksheet and rank-order the items that are checked (SUDS 20 or higher) from least to most fearful.

Psychoeducation

What Interoceptive Exercises Are Designed to Accomplish

"We can look at panic as a phobia of internal sensations. Besides having fearful thoughts in panic, you may also have been conditioned to fear the sensations. Just as people often want to avoid exposure to feared *external* situations, you may want to avoid exposure to feared *internal* sensations. While you cannot run away from your own body, you may have tried to find ways so as not to feel the sensations you fear. Some people avoid exercising, saunas, caffeine, being out on a hot day, exciting events, heated discussions, and so forth.

"One of the best ways to work on the conditioned fear of panic attacks is through what we call *interoceptive exposure*. 'Interoceptive' simply means feedback we get from within our bodies. We are going to do little exercises that bring on sensations similar to those in panic and have you repeat them till you no longer fear them. Just as with *in vivo* exposure in phobias, your fear will diminish as you repeat these exercises. The goal is to diminish the fear you feel when these bodily sensations occur in a panic. After doing any given exercise, you can apply the coping tools you have learned (diaphragmatic breathing and/or challenging fearful automatic thoughts) to help you handle the sensations."

Symptoms Commmonly Elicited by Interoceptive Exercises: This list describes the sensations most commonly elicited by various exercises. However, any given exercise may produce different or additional symptoms. This is why the instructions state that you must *not* tell your client what sensations to expect. Doing so would pose an unnecessary restriction on the client's reactions or scare the client more than necessary.

- Shake head side to side (Dizziness)
- Place head between legs (Dizziness)
- Run in place (Heart palpitations)
- Tense body completely (Chest tension)
- Hold breath (Tight chest, suffocation)
- Spin (Dizziness)
- Breathe through a small straw (Suffocation, shortness of breath)
- Hyperventilate (Light-headed, faint feeling)
- Place external pressure on throat (Suffocation, lump in throat)
- Stare at a spot: wall, mirror, or hand (Depersonalization, derealization)
- Swallow quickly (Lump in throat)
- Focus on worst sensation in imagery: throat closing (Lack of air), heart pumping (Pain and discomfort), etc.
- Use a tongue depressor (Choking)
- Put pressure to upper arm (Numbness, tingling)
- Press upper arm against torso (Numbness, tingling)
- Stand up suddenly from a lying down position (Dizziness)

Exclusions. While the listed exercises are not dangerous, actually quite harmless, clients with certain conditions will be asked to be excluded. The primary reason is to prevent a medical condition from becoming aggravated. Clients may be excluded who have:

- Epilepsy or other history of seizures
- Moderate to severe asthma
- Chronic arrythmia or fibrillations
- Moderate to severe lung or heart problems
- History of fainting and/or *very* low blood pressure
- Pregnancy

If there is any question regarding the medical condition of a client, your client should ask his or her physician. Other situations arise requiring good judgment. For example, if a client has a very bad neck or back, certain exercises may be unrealistic for him or her to do, such as sitting with the head between the legs or spinning while standing up (sometimes they can spin in a spinning chair instead). If a client does have a medical condition, you may still try to find exercises that he or she can do (see below).

Exercises Nearly Everyone Can Do Safely
In the office:

- Hold breath
- External pressure on throat
- Stare at a spot
- Use a tongue depressor
- Swallow quickly
- Focus on your worst sensation using imagery
- Apply pressure to upper arm
- Press upper arm against torso

Outside the office (Some of these exercises can also be done in the office):

- Ingest caffeine: coffee, black tea, sodas with caffeine, chocolate
- Relax and daydream
- Create heat: turn up heat in house or car and sit with very hot clothing and the windows closed
- Wear tight clothing around the neck
- Go into a small, dark closet, close the door, and stay inside

Skill Building

Identifying Feared Interoceptive Exercises

The exercises to be done in the office are listed in table 7.1. Additional exercises and those to be done in naturalistic situations are listed in table 9.2 (session 9). The first step is to go through all or most of the exercises listed in Worksheet 7: Interoceptive Exposure Record. I keep the worksheet and rank-order those exercises that have SUDS scores of 20 or higher from least to most fearful.

Supplies Needed

1. *Timer.* You want a timer that sounds an alarm when the time is up. If you attempt to use a watch or a clock, it is distracting during most exercises, e.g., when spinning (you almost have to stop in order to look at a clock). Furthermore, you do not want to convey the message to the client that he or she should anxiously watch the clock tick.

2. *Worksheet 7:* Interoceptive Exposure Record, pad, and pen.

Table 7.1: Interoceptive Exercises for the Office

Exercise	Length of Time*	Instructions
1. Shake head side to side	30 sec.	Lower your head a *bit* and shake it loosely from side to side, with your eyes open. When the timer goes off, *suddenly* lift your head and stare straight ahead for a little while.
2. Head between legs	1.5 min.	Sit in a straight chair. Bend your head down between your legs, trying to keep it lower than your heart level. When the timer goes off, *suddenly* lift your head and stare straight ahead for a little while.
3. Run in place	1 min.	Jog in place lifting your legs to hip level, if possible. (Or run up stairs.)
4. Complete body tension	1 min.	While sitting, make fists with your hands, tense your feet, bring your shoulders forward and tense your chest and entire body. If possible, stretch out your legs while holding the tension. Breathe deeply throughout.
5. Hold breath	30 sec.	Just as you begin timing, take a deep breath, cover your nose and mouth with your hand, and try to hold it for 30 sec. *If you cannot hold for that length of time, stop earlier.*
6. Spin	(a) 1 min. (b) 1 min. and walk	Spin around at a good pace. Give yourself room and have a wall nearby to put your hand against if you lose your balance. Or use an office chair that spins and push against the floor as you spin.
7. Straw breathing	2 min.	Place a thin straw in your mouth and breathe in and out through it. Pinch your nose *slightly* with your other hand. If there is too much pressure, after a while, let go of your nose before stopping altogether.

* Do (a) first and keep repeating it until your SUDS level is less than 20. Then do (b), and keep repeating until your SUDS level is less than 20.

Continued on next page

Table 7.1: Interoceptive Exercises for the Office (cont.)

Exercise	Length of Time	Instructions
8. Hyperventilate	1.5 min.	While *standing*, breathe deeply in and out through your *mouth* (like panting, but slower, and breathing *out* more than breathing *in*). Make it audible, i.e., make a sound that can be heard across the room.
9. External pressure on throat	1 min.	Using either your thumb or two fingers, apply pressure to the middle of your throat. Apply pressure until it feels uncomfortable, but not extremely so.
10. Stare at a spot	2 min.	Pick a spot on an empty wall and stare at it *without deviating your gaze* at all.
11. Quick swallowing	4 times	Swallow as quickly as you can four times in a row.
12. Focus on your worst sensation in imagery	2 min.	Remember your worst panic sensation. Now close your eyes, imagine a very bad panic, and totally focus on that feared symptom. Or think of a feared thought or image, such as your "losing control" or "going insane" (imagining yourself in an insane asylum), etc. Do not allow yourself to be distracted.

3. *Coffee stirrers or cocktail straws.* These are thin straws, often striped red and white, with a tiny hole. A regular straw would defeat the purpose of the test because the opening is too large. There is, however, a large variation among coffee stirrers. Those that have a division in the middle, two tiny holes, are usually too small. Many have slightly larger holes, which makes the breathing much easier. (Three millimeters inside diameter is just right for this purpose.)

Specific Instructions for Interoceptive Exposures

1. Do not tell your client what sensations to expect. Some exercises produce sensations while the person is in the process of doing them; others are felt right after stopping. Therefore, right after finishing the exercises, have the client sit (or stand) for a few seconds while paying attention to the sensations produced and any anxiety. The anxiety can be brought on by the sensations or by just engaging in the exercises.

2. Encourage your client to stay with the full time allotted for each exercise. However, if too uncomfortable, he or she can stop before the allotted time.

3. Have your client use the Subjective Units of Anxiety-Distress Scale (SUDS) from 0 to 100 to describe the level of anxiety experienced. Help your client distinguish between physical *discomfort* and *anxiety/fear*. The sensations produced can be very intense, creating a great deal of discomfort, but your client must assess the presence of any anxiety/fear associated with doing the exercises or the sensations produced. Thus, after your client is clear on what sensations and anxiety level were experienced, he or she should record these in Worksheet 7 before proceeding to the next exercise.

4. Some clients say with dismay that the sensations produced were exactly like those experienced in a panic. Their SUDS level may be as high as 80 or even higher. In response, I tell them, "This is actually very good—not that I wish you discomfort, but now we have at least one exercise that we know is particularly relevant for you; now we have something concrete to work with. As you keep practicing the exercise and watch your fear diminish, it will provide you with some very powerful learning." The aim is to feel the sensations to the fullest, and the more similar to a panic sensation they are, the better.

5. Always do the exercises with your client the first time. This helps your client feel less awkward since you are not sitting idly by, and it is much more likely that he or she will do the exercises up to the time limit. It also shows that you are not afraid of the sensations. (Practice doing them *before* you see your first client so that you will know what to expect.)

6. In order to get through the entire list of twelve exercises, you need to keep very focused on the task. Right after recording the sensations felt and the SUDS level, ask your client to briefly share these, and then go to the next exercise. A lengthy discussion serves more as an avoidance.

Summary of Session

"Today we have worked on identifying which exercises bring on symptoms that you respond to with fear. Now we know which ones we need to work on. I will keep the worksheet for this week and rank-order the exercises you need to work on. You will be repeating the ones that are relevant for you until you no longer fear them."

Feedback from Client

"What questions, aside from what you brought up earlier, do you have about what we reviewed today? Are there any related issues you wish to address?"

Difficulties You May Encounter

Your Client Resists the Interoceptive Exercises

Client: I don't want to feel anything like panic sensations. Why should I bring them on?

Therapist This is very understandable. If I were in your shoes, I'd probably feel the same. However, this provides a unique opportunity to learn that the sensations do not produce harm. I am here, and I'll be doing each exercise with you, exactly as you will be doing.

Client: I'm still afraid.

Therapist Your fear and apprehension are understandable, because this happens in panic disorder. However, avoiding the sensations serves the same function as avoiding phobic situations. This won't help you overcome your panic disorder. We will take a step at a time. The first exercise is shaking the head back and forth like this (demonstrate). Would this exercise be too hard for you to do?

Client: No.

Therapist Good. If the sensations produced by an exercise become too scary, you can stop before the time is up. Do you have any other questions? Shall we proceed?

In group work, people seem particularly eager to participate. This occurs even with those who have medical conditions. We may negotiate around the exercises that they can do.

Homework

The homework for session 8 is as follows:

1. Worksheet 1: Panic Frequency and Intensity.

2. Read session 7 in the client manual and bring up any questions or comments.

3. Continue to make entries in Worksheet 6: Core Belief Log. Please bring them in next time. (If relevant, pursue weekly the percentage on the evidence continuum.)

If agoraphobia is present:

4. Exposures (for the client to record on Worksheet 10 and you on Therapist Record 10T, under "Planned Exposures"). This homework was probably set in the beginning of the session.

Worksheet 7: Interoceptive Exposure Record

Name: _____ Date: _____

SUDS: Subjective Units of Anxiety-Distress Scale

0 = Totally calm, no anxiety/fear
50 = Moderate level of anxiety/fear
100 = Intolerable level of anxiety/fear

Exercise	Describe Any Sensations Felt	SUDS	Check if SUDS ≥ 20
Shake head, 30 sec.			
Head down, 1.5 min.			
Run in place, 1 min.			
Body tension, 1 min.			
Hold breath, 30 sec.			
Spin, 1 min.			
Straw breathing, 2 min.			
Hyperventilation, 1.5 min.			
Throat pressure, 1 min.			
Stare at spot, 2 min.			
Quick swallowing, 4 times			
Sensation in imagery, 2 min.			

Session 8

Interoceptive Exposure: Repeating Fear-Provoking Exercises

Monitoring of Current Status

Review Worksheet 1: Panic Frequency and Intensity. Proceed as in session 1.

Agenda

Before this session, you will have rank-ordered (from 1 up) the interoceptive exercises that produced a SUDS level of 20 or higher. In the session, you will work with your client on the exercises, starting with the exercise ranked number one. If all your client's SUDS were below 20, you can have your client work with some of these exercises, even though they seemed to produce little fear. (Alternately, you may explore exercises from table 9.2.)

Review of Homework

The homework assignments that you are following up since session 7 are:

1. Worksheet 1: Panic Frequency and Intensity.

2. Reading session 7 in the client manual.

3. Entries from Worksheet 6: Core Belief Log.

If agoraphobia is present:

4. Exposures as recorded on Worksheet 10, "Actual Effort." Plan new exposures with your client.

Concepts and Skills

Skill Building

Repeating Feared Interoceptive Exercises

You will use Worksheet 8: Repeating Interoceptive Exercises to record your client's responses. (You may use a copy rather than your client's book.) In this worksheet, you no longer write down the client's sensations (which was done in session 7), but only the SUDS level. That is, record the date, write down the exercise being worked on, and the SUDS level.

Supplies Needed

1. *Timer.* (If you are working with a group, you would ideally have several timers available, one for each pair of people working together.)

2. *Worksheet 8:* Repeating Interoceptive Exercises, pad and pen.

3. *Coffee stirrers or cocktail straws.*

Instructions: "We are now going to repeat the exercises you found fear-provoking the last time, starting with the easiest one. I will coach you, but I will no longer do the exercise with you. Allow yourself to feel the sensations fully; pay attention to them. In other words, I will ask you not to use distraction or otherwise to minimize the sensations, because then the work will not mean much. This is like any exposure—it works best when one confronts the fear to the fullest. While you are doing the exercise and right after you finish, pay attention to the anxiety/fear you feel, expressed in SUDS. Are you ready? The first-ranked exercise to work on is _____ ." (Time the client.)

Afterwards ask your client for his or her SUDS level. Then ask you client: "What was going on in your mind, what thoughts/images did you have?" Any negative automatic thoughts are now challenged, following Worksheet 4, but verbally:

- What is your exact automatic thought?

- How likely is it that your feared thought will occur? Use the scale from 0 to 100 percent.

- What is your evidence that _____ will happen?

- How can you refute it?

- What are alternative hypotheses? What is the probability of each?

- Now, if you were to face up to your original automatic thought, how could you do it?

- What is the probability of it being true *now*, 0 to 100 percent?

On the other hand, if your client's SUDS level is much lower, find out what is different and what the client is learning.

Repeat each exercise up to three times in a row until the SUDS drops to below 20, always challenging the fears. If still high, nonetheless stop for now and give it as a homework assignment. Then move to your client's second-ranked exercise and do the same. As soon as your client does an exercise easily, see if there is a way to increase the challenge a bit. For instance, you may ask your client to walk right after he or she stops spinning, unless the person is too off balance and might fall. Right after holding the breath the person might be asked to hyperventilate a few times.

Summary of Session

"Today we have repeated interoceptive exercises that produced fear in you. Your fear diminished to some extent as a result of the repetition. Furthermore, now you will be asked to start doing them in other situations."

Feedback from Client

"What questions, aside from what you brought up earlier, do you have about what we reviewed today? Are there any related issues you wish to address?"

Difficulties You May Encounter

The Office/Clinic Feels Too Safe to Do the Exercises

Client:	I don't have anxiety doing these exercises here, because I'm in your office/the clinic. It feels safe here.
Therapist:	One thing we can do is have you imagine you have the sensation outside of here. Can you try?
Client:	Yes.

After doing some exercises:

Therapist:	Your SUDS continue to be very low. Is it still because you feel safe here?
Client:	Yes.
Therapist:	That's okay. We'll finish with the rest of the exercises. Then I'll have you do them at home alone and later in other places.
Client:	That may be too scary.
Therapist:	Okay, you can do them with a coach present, if you have someone who is not afraid of these exercises and sensations. Then have your coach just be in another room while you do the exercise.

If the client does not have an available coach and is home alone:

Therapist: Try then for a very short time. For example, spinning, try it for fifteen seconds instead of one minute. Remember to have a wall nearby first in case you lose your balance. As soon as you are a bit more confident, do it for longer times, up to the time limit, and even try to walk right after you stop.

The Exercise Does Not Bring on the Expected Fear

If your client is very fearful of a particular sensation, but the exercise(s) that is expected to bring on this sensation produces low SUDS levels, you may want to ask your client to demonstrate how he or she does the exercise. You might discover that your client is finding a way around the exercise, so it produces a minimal effect. In this case, you demonstrate again, remind your client that it will not work unless he or she gives his all, and have him or her repeat it.

Homework

The homework for session 9 is as follows:

1. Worksheet 1: Panic Frequency and Intensity.

2. Read session 8 in the client manual and bring up any questions or comments.

3. Continue to make entries in Worksheet 6: Core Belief Log.

4. The interoceptive assignment for the next session is to *repeat all interoceptives with a SUDS level of 20 or higher daily, three times in a row.* "I will ask you to do them even if your fear went down while doing them with me. My presence, as well you being here in my office may have made you feel safe, constituting a safety signal. Remember, this needs to be expanded to other situations for it to work. Use Worksheet 7 as a reference, and record the exercises you work on in Worksheet 8. If you find an exercise particularly fear-provoking, we can do it again here, in the next session. Whether you use Worksheet 8 in the book or copies of it, you must remember to bring them in to the next session. Only this way will I be able to follow your progress and know what to concentrate on in the next session."

5. An associated part of the interoceptive homework is to fill out two samples of Worksheet 4: Challenging Automatic Thoughts as pertaining to the fears, no matter how slight, brought on by doing the interoceptives.

If agoraphobia is present:

6. Exposures (for the client to record on Worksheet 10 and you on Therapist Record 10T, under "Planned Exposures"). This homework was probably set in the beginning of the session.

Worksheet 8: Repeating Interoceptive Exercises

Name of person doing the exercises: _____

Use this column first

Date	Exercise being worked on	SUDS

Then use this column

Date	Exercise being worked on	SUDS

COACH: Guide the person doing the exercises.

Before exercise: • Allow yourself to feel the sensations fully; pay attention to them.

After exercise: • What was your SUDS level?

• What was going on in your mind, your thoughts/images?

Challenge any negative Automatic Thoughts/Images!

• What is your evidence that _____ would happen?

• What are alternative thoughts (positive thoughts)?

If lower SUDS than previously:

• What do you think you are learning?

Repeat exercise till SUDS is less than 20. Stop any given exercise after three trials. Repeat exercise on other days, in other places.

Session 9

Interoceptive Exposure: New Situations and Naturalistic Interoceptives

Monitoring of Current Status

Review Worksheet 1: Panic Frequency and Intensity. Proceed as in session 1.

Agenda

After reviewing your client's progress, you will have a good idea how much work there is still to be done. Keep working on interoceptives that produce SUDS levels of 20 or above. Now it is also time to expand the assignment to other, more challenging situations, and to have your client seek out more naturalistic exposures. You will now also plan with your client to do interoceptives in agoraphobic situations.

Review of Homework

The homework assignments that you are following up since session 8 are:

1. Worksheet 1: Panic Frequency and Intensity.

2. Reading session 8 in the client manual.

3. Entries from Worksheet 6: Core Belief Log.

4. Worksheet 8: Repeating Interoceptive Exercises.

5. Two samples of Worksheet 4: Challenging Automatic Thoughts as pertaining to the fears brought on when doing interoceptive exercises.

If agoraphobia is present:

6. Exposures as recorded on Worksheet 10, "Actual Effort." Plan new exposures with your client. (Observe that from now on, your client is to include interoceptives in feared situations, to be recorded on Worksheet 8.)

Concepts and Skills

Skill Building

Doing the Interoceptives in New Situations

Your client has done the interoceptives at home. Now it is time to plan to expand these exercises further. One of the best places for a few of the exercises is in a parked car. I would naturally emphasize to the client *not* to do them while driving. However, in a parked car the client can hyperventilate, hold his or her breath, and breathe through a straw. The person can also do interoceptives in other people's homes, e.g., that of a close friend or relative. They could be done in their bathroom, bedroom, or other place.

There is no limit to the creativity in expanding the exercises. Other possibilities of expansion are, e.g., wearing a sweater in a warm restaurant, alternately tensing and relaxing the arms while driving, etc. A good interoceptive exposure is to quietly spin with one's clothes on in a fitting room and then walk out to the store aisles. This could mimic feelings of dizziness brought on by anxiety when the person is in stores. While alone in an elevator, the person could hold his or her breath or hyperventilate. One could hold one's breath while standing in line.

It is exceedingly helpful if you can do some of these exercises with your client in a setting other than your office. If there is an elevator, a staircase, a hallway in your building, or a parking structure, take a few minutes before the end of the session to do them there. In these cases, it is imperative that you do the exercises as well. A direct behavioral experience is much more powerful than simply discussing it.

All interoceptives are to be recorded on Worksheet 8. Under "Exercise being worked on," your client can write down the exercise and the place, e.g., "Hyperventilating in a parked car," "Holding breath while standing in line," etc.

Naturalistic Interoceptives

Give your client also the task to do more "naturalistic" interoceptives, i.e., those that we encounter in normal life. A number of those are listed in table 9.1. That is, the more activities that bring on feared sensations are sought out, the better. Again, instruct your client to record them on Worksheet 8.

If fear continues, your client must continue to practice on interoceptives. Furthermore, if at any time from this point on the client expresses fear of a symptom, ask him or her to repeat the relevant exercise anew.

Interoceptives in Agoraphobic Situations

Dr. David Barlow, at his presentation at Northern California Kaiser (October 1998), emphasized the need for clients to do interoceptive exposures in essentially every agoraphobic situation. Your client has done *in vivo* exposures all along in the treatment. Now, from the ninth session on, a new challenge will be added to those situations: doing interoceptives. You will systematically add interoceptives to each agoraphobic assignment you plan with your client. If a phobia has been totally overcome, it can still be repeated, along with an appropriate interoceptive.

As already mentioned, when the fear pertains to driving, you can have your client tense up the arms and relax, wear a warm sweater with the windows closed and the heater on, etc. In contrast, you would not ask your client to hyperventilate, hold his or her breath, or breathe through a straw while driving, but they can be done in a parked car. As also mentioned, some interoceptives can be done while standing in line and using elevators. If a person fears cinemas, one can hold one's breath or breathe through a straw (no one would know why the person was holding a small straw between his or her lips). It helps to be creative.

All these interoceptive exposures can be recorded on Worksheet 8. Again, the exercise and the place can be recorded. The exercises should be repeated until the sensation no longer produces fear in that particular situation.

Table 9.1: Naturalistic Interoceptive Exercises[*]

Exercise	Length of Time[*]	Instructions
13. Ingest caffeine[†]	(a) Coffee (b) Coffee & chocolate	Drink a cup of caffeinated coffee or tea (rather strong). For part (b) either drink two cups or combine one cup with a piece of chocolate. Here you want to work on sensations brought on by caffeine. One advantage is that the maximum effect of the caffeine is not immediate, allowing you to practice with greater unpredictability.

[*] Many of the exercises are from Drs. Barlow and Craske, as mentioned. Numbers 20 and 21 were demonstrated by Dr. Alec Pollard in a workshop at the 1995 conference of the Anxiety Disorders Association of America.

[†] Many panickers stop drinking coffee or tea for fear of the sensations produced. The idea here is not to get your client back to ingesting caffeine on a regular basis, but it is good to learn not to be afraid of it.

Continued on the following page

Exercise	Length of Time	Instructions
14. Relax and daydream	(a) 5 min. (b) 10 min.	Sit and try to relax. Allow yourself just to daydream without focusing on anything planned or anything that needs your attention.
15. Create heat	(a) 15 min. (b) 30 min.	Turn up the heat at home and sit with your warmest clothing on. In the car, close the window and turn up the heat, especially on a hot day (if too fear-provoking, start with 5 min.). This is a very powerful exercise for those fearing heat and suffocation.
16. Stare at your mirror image and/or at the palm of your hand	(a) 2 min. (b) 3 min.	Stare at one spot on your person in the mirror or at a spot on your palm 6–8 inches from your face *without deviating your gaze* at all.
17. Tight clothing around neck	(a) 30 min. (b) 1 min.	Wear something tight around your neck, i.e., a scarf or collar.
18. Vertigo	(a) 30 sec. (b) 1 min.	Stand by a *tall* building and look up at its exterior wall.
19. Crawl under the bed	5–15 min.	Try to create an experience of being closed in.
20. Pressure to upper arm	1 min.	Raise one arm at the elbow. With your other hand apply pressure to your upper arm, so the circulation is restricted.
21. Upper arm against torso	1 min.	With one arm hanging loosely at your side, grasp your upper arm with the opposite hand. Grip the upper arm tightly, and press and turn it firmly against your torso.
22. Hyperventilate and hold breath	1 min.	Do the hyperventilation exercise for one min. and immediately hold your breath briefly.
23. Stand up suddenly		Stand up suddenly from a lying down position.
24. Run up stairs	Up to 5 min.	Run up a few flights of stairs.
25. Vigorous exercise	15 to 30 min.	Do aerobics or other vigorous exercise for 15 to 30 min., depending on your stamina. (If you exercise regularly, this may not be an interoceptive challenge.)

Exercise	Length of Time	Instructions
26. Sauna	5–20 min.	Sit in a sauna for varying lengths of time.
27. Intense emotions	1–2 hours	Watch something suspenseful (mystery movie, sports event).
28. Intense excitement		Go on an amusement park ride.
29. Pillow over face	1 to 5 min.	Excellent exercise for someone who fears suffocation.
30. Sit in dark closet with door(s) closed	1 to 15 min.	As above.

Summary of Session

"Today we have explored new situations where you can practice at least some of the interoceptive exercises. We also looked at expanding to more naturalistic activities. We identified some of the specific situations where you will be doing exercises. Finally, from now on, when you do *in vivo* exposures, you will need to add interoceptive exercises."

Feedback from Client

"What questions, aside from what you brought up earlier, do you have about what we reviewed today? Are there any related issues you wish to address?"

Difficulties You May Encounter

Your Client Resists Doing the Interoceptives When Out and About

If your client expresses hesitation about this, listen first to the objection or hesitation. Explore the reasons. Your client might feel self-conscious. Walk your client through such social fears.

Client: I'd be too embarrassed doing these exercises, like hyperventilating in a car.

Therapist: Remember to do this only in a *parked* car. Well, tell you what. You can first do it while parked in an isolated place, where no one sees you. If you fear people seeing you do it, I would not ask you to do it in such places, but if you didn't mind a passerby noticing you doing it, the more power to you! I would not ask you to do interoceptives anywhere where I would not be willing to do them. For instance, I'd never purposefully hyperventilate while standing in line.

It is also likely that your client simply fears feeling the sensations.

Client: I'm just too afraid feeling the sensations when I'm out on my own.

Therapist: Let's take small steps again. How do you think you'll feel holding your breath while standing in line, for about fifteen to twenty seconds?

Client: That'd be okay.

Therapist: Fine, start with that. If you were driving, would you be afraid of alternately tensing and relaxing your arm muscles? I bet this tensing and/or relaxing your arms has happened naturally to you while driving. I certainly have been in driving situations when I tensed up a lot. At other times I have concentrated on relaxing my arms. So you see, we don't need to make this too hard or too complicated. But, as behavioral experiments, these are powerful bits of evidence showing that your behavior is under your control, even when very anxious.

Consider doing some interoceptives with the client outside the office, if you have not already done so. A very good option is to use one or two entire sessions to do guided mastery exposure, where you accompany your client to do *in vivo* exposures. You can guide your client with the external exposure, as well as do interoceptives with them and then have your client do them alone. Short of that, if you are absolutely limited to the office, keep doing the exposures in the office and instruct your client to do them at home until that becomes comfortable.

Homework

The homework for session 10 is as follows:

1. Worksheet 1: Panic Frequency and Intensity.

2. Read session 9 in your book and bring up any questions or comments.

3. Continue to make entries in Worksheet 6: Core Belief Log.

4. Continue recording interoceptives in Worksheet 8. This time, in the space designated "Exercise being worked on," write down the exercise and where you did it. Again, make sure to bring in Worksheet 8 to the next session for me to follow your progress.

5. Bring in again two samples of Worksheet 4: Challenging Automatic Thoughts as pertaining to the fears brought about by doing the interoceptives. (They could be in agoraphobic situations.) If you happened to have very little fear doing them, please nonetheless fill out those two worksheets.

If agoraphobia is present:

6. Exposures (for the client to record on Worksheet 10 and you on Therapist Record 10T, under "Planned Exposures"). This homework was probably set in the beginning of the session.

Adjuncts to Success: Strategies to Deal with Chronic Worry, Learning to Be Assertive

Monitoring of Current Status

Review Worksheet 1: Panic Frequency and Intensity. Proceed as in session 1.

Agenda

At this juncture in the treatment it is good to review what has been accomplished. If your client continues to be very fearful of panic attacks, you may need to continue working on the fearful cognitions and interoceptive exposures. You will not do your client a service to embark on new problem areas if your client needs more direct work on fears.

On the other hand, if your client's progress is good and strong, and like many panickers, he or she has issues with chronic worry or assertiveness, you can work on these areas. The lack of assertiveness is paramount in many clients with panic disorder and agoraphobia. Here, you will help your client review the areas in which there is a problem with assertiveness and look for ways to deal with it.

If you determine during the assessment and the first couple of sessions that chronic worry is a major issue, your client's panic disorder is less prominent, and there is no or very mild agoraphobia, you may choose to work on worry strategies in parallel with the panic work. This is only possible if there are no other issues demanding the time and attention from the sessions. In this case, you can cover one to two strategies per session and have your client try them out during the week, along with other assignments. You can similarly work with assertiveness issues earlier than the tenth session if your client is progressing fast with the panic work and no other major issues have surfaced. In these cases, you can discuss with your client the option of working on these problem areas. That is, it is better to have such agendas instead of your client merely trying to fill out time with an update on his/her general life, especially if not relevant for treatment success. As mentioned in the beginning, however, you must be very observant of what the client's problems are and make an explicit agreement about what you will focus on. Hence, if panic disorder is the major problem, that needs to be addressed first.

Review of Homework

The homework assignments that you are following up since session 9 are:

1. Worksheet 1: Panic Frequency and Intensity.

2. Read session 9 in the client manual.

3. Entries from Worksheet 6: Core Belief Log.

4. Worksheet 8: Repeating Interoceptive Exercises.

5. Two samples of Worksheet 4: Challenging Automatic Thoughts as pertaining to the fears brought on when doing interoceptive exercises.

If agoraphobia is present:

6. Exposures as recorded on Worksheet 10, "Actual Effort." Plan new exposures with your client.

Concepts and Skills

A number of panickers, when asked, say that they have been chronic worriers for years. They may say, "I have worried for as long as I can remember." "I have always been a worrywart." However, if not having worried before, many panickers become worriers *after* having developed panic disorder. They do not just worry about having another panic attack again, but about many other things as well. They feel they change: they are generally more apprehensive, view the world as a less safe place, and view themselves as unable to cope with anxiety in general.

Some clients worry continuously about impending disaster. Those who expect disaster worry as a means of preparation for the bad event. They think that they *cannot cope* if something bad happened *unexpectedly*, and/or they think that if they worry enough, the disaster will not occur (this is the maladaptive thought "disaster expectation," covered in session 4). There are specific strategies that can be used to cope with the general worry. In order to have a positive effect, these require work on the part of your client.

Panic disorder does not occur in a vacuum. It is naturally connected to unique biological and psychological events in the individual. People may be overwhelmed by their own emotions and/or they do not stand up to others when they need to. In this vein, panic and phobias may be a vehicle to avoid facing other real-life issues. Often, these may be worse fears in life, at least as perceived by the particular individual. Also, the person may be "locked" and inflexible, and thus not find a way of dealing with other people. For example, if a person has learned that he or she should not set limits with others and fears his or her own guilt feelings if doing so, there may simply be no way out of a difficult internal dilemma. Standing up to others involves true risk because the other person may react in a rejecting way. Thus, nonassertiveness is not exercising control in an interpersonal situation. This leads to feelings of helplessness, which in turn can increase anxiety, hopelessness, and/or depression. In contrast, assertiveness brings about a sense of mastery and self-worth.

Skill Building

Strategies for Dealing with Chronic Worry

Distinguishing between what you can and you cannot control. Many clients do not keep apart what they can from what they cannot control. That is, they view things they cannot control as if they could control them. This creates difficulties again and again. There are many things that we as single individuals cannot control at all, like the weather, traffic, our heredity, and so on. Many things people might be able to exercise *some* control over. Good examples of the latter are how we might attempt to *influence* other people's behaviors and decisions. You can do this by asking them to change their behavior in an assertive message, by giving your opinion about their choices, etc. Certainly parents to adult children often hope to continue shaping their children's choices. However, it is exceedingly helpful to keep in mind that you ultimately have no control over other people's lives and choices. (Obviously, in a marriage or family setting, there is a great deal of compromising and anguish that goes into finding a way of living together that is acceptable and tolerable to all involved.)

In sum, if you *can* exercise some control, do you know what it consists of and are you willing to relinquish control over the things you cannot control? Though much easier said than done, it is a worthwhile issue to work on.

Moving from fear and worry to action. The very best of all strategies for dealing with worry is to take some action that counters the feared event. The wisdom of this strategy is that the action will help absorb the anxiety. A recent example came up with a client. My client was in the process of moving, and a few days before the movers were to come, he started to worry intensely whether the movers would show up or not. Having learned to work with the worry strategies, he decided to take the one action he could, which was to call the company to verify that they had him on their schedule and were planning to come. This made him feel much better. He recognized that he had ultimately no guarantee that they would come, i.e., he did not have ultimate control over their actions. Yet he decided that if they did not show up, he would have tried his best, and it would not be absolute disaster. He and his family would find another solution, one way or another.

Challenging worrisome automatic thoughts. Taking action, the strategy described above, is a *behavioral* way of dealing with worry. The best *cognitive* strategy is to challenge the worrisome thoughts just as you taught your client to do earlier with the automatic thoughts pertaining to specific panic fears (Worksheet 4: Challenging Automatic Thoughts). The first step is to recognize the exact automatic thought associated with the worry and then challenge it.

The client can achieve this awareness by paying attention to their automatic thoughts during the day, by asking oneself what the thoughts were right before a change in emotions, by asking what the expectations are *vis-à-vis* a new situation, etc. Excellent questions are "What am I afraid of right now?" "What's the worst that could happen?" "What exactly am I worried about?"

Confronting "what ifs." Most worry thoughts start with "What if . . . ?" The worst is to leave it unanswered. It always seems to imply a catastrophic outcome. Instead, these "what ifs" should be answered: "Okay, let's assume X will happen. What then?" When answering it, the person should always think of coping strategies. The feared event is almost never as disastrous as the mere question "What if?" implies, and even if it is, it's better to confront it. Examples are: "What if I can't pay the bills?" "What if my alcoholic father ruins the holiday again?" If the feared event is truly "catastrophic" such as death, repeated, prolonged exposure is nonetheless the answer. The person describes the feared scene repeatedly in writing with the inclusion of all possible details. This may take from half an hour to forty-five minutes each time. This approach helps decatastrophize the feared event.

Scheduling worry time. If a person worries for an hour or more a day, and/or if the worry feels consuming and distressing, scheduling "worry time" is an excellent strategy. It only works if done tightly, without loopholes. The worry time should be preferably the same time every day, or at a certain time on weekdays and another on weekends. The amount of time can vary from fifteen minutes to one hour per day, depending on how much time the client usually spends worrying. The length of the worry time should always be less than that baseline.

During the worry time the person sits down with a paper and pen and no distractions. He or she does nothing but worry about the feared event(s). The paper and pen are to write down the worry and any possible solutions. If no solution can be found, the person can write down the worry, its outcome, and the thoughts and emotions. If the client gets distracted, every effort should be made to return to the worries. (The paper and pen help to keep focused.) Once the worry time is over (a timer could announce it), the person should leave the worries and look for distraction from them in any way possible. (The worry time should not be just before bedtime, because it is much harder to turn the worry off.) When a worrisome thought arises any other time of the day or night, the person is to jot it down so as not to forget it and save it for the next worry time.

Thought stopping. Thought stopping is probably one of the weaker strategies but is sometimes useful and can be effective *in conjunction with* any of the strategies listed above. It is useful when the same negative thought pops up again and again, there is no solution to the problem, or the worrisome thought is overly persistent.

Once aware of the thought, the person says, "Stop!" emphatically. It can be said loudly at home or in the car, otherwise subliminally, and/or the person may envision a stop sign. The person then changes the thought to something else. Of course, the unwanted thought soon returns. The thought-stopping technique works only if it is repeated over and over, as soon as the person becomes aware of the unwanted thought. After many repetitions the negative thought should subside.

Putting on the rose-colored glasses. This is a term used by Sobel and Ornstein in their book *The Healthy Mind, Healthy Body Handbook* (1996). Since people cannot see reality exactly as it is, they might as well see it in a positive rather than a negative light, i. e., through rose-colored glasses. Optimism and pessimism are learned habits, and optimistic thinking has a positive impact on emotional and physical health. To practice seeing life with an optimistic outlook, it's important to stay in the present, to reflect on good rather than bad past experiences, and to celebrate one's accomplishments. For my pessimistic clients I recommend Seligman's book *Learned Optimism* (1990).

Strategies for Dealing with Stress

Limiting stress that is under one's control. All of us create stress for ourselves. If it takes the form of challenges, this might be very positive. People create undue stress in their lives when they ignore what else is happening in their lives, when they follow *shoulds, oughts, and musts* rather than what they themselves truly want.

Relaxation. Learning progressive muscle relaxation can significantly reduce tension. It serves as a positive coping skill. An excellent book from which to learn relaxation methods is *The Relaxation and Stress Reduction Workbook*, Fourth Edition by Davis, Robbins-Eshelman, and McKay (1995).

Exercise: One way to enhance biological toughness to stress, as well as to improve our physical and mental well-being, is physical exercise. Aerobic exercise, which is any exercise that stimulates the cardiovascular system, produces sympathetic nervous system arousal. When the person exercises regularly, adrenaline and noradrenaline are used, depleted, and built up again. This has a positive impact on the system.

Fun and humor: Clients can benefit from bringing balance to their lives by including entertainment, fun, and humor. It is especially helpful if they find and make time for an activity which they thoroughly enjoy. It is also helpful to plan these for after an expected rough time.

Skill Building

Strategies for Dealing with Nonassertion

Taking care of oneself and recognizing the rights of others: Many people view themselves as selfish if they exert their wishes. Yet taking care of oneself does not imply stepping on others. A excellent book is *Self-Assertion for Women* by Pamela Butler (1992).

The main goal of assertiveness is expressing oneself. While standing up to others does not guarantee a desired outcome, the probability of getting what we want is greatly increased if we verbalize it. Ultimately, the greatest value is in speaking up. Even if one does not get what one wants, the person feels much better having expressed himself or herself and at least having tried to influence the other person.

Knowing what you want, but not having to justify it. It is important to state what you want in a clear way in order to get your point across. The fewer words are used in the assertive message, the better. The message does not get as easily lost. When the person you are talking to does not seem to listen, use the broken record technique, i.e., repeat the same request over and over with minor or no modifications.

"I" vs. "you" statements. People who are unassertive often fear being aggressive. One simple way of keeping the distinction between an assertive and an aggressive message is to use the word "I." As long as "I" statements are used, the less likely that one is attacking the other person. In contrast, "you" statements, especially using "you" in the beginning of a sentence, are often associated with criticism or attack of the other person.

Making a request. Sometimes just saying "no" is the most appropriate course of action. However, it is often very helpful to make a request of what is desired as well. It adds great clarity to state the desired alternative outcome or behavior. This applies as much to a business transaction (asking for a refund) as to a personal situation.

Teaching others how you like to be treated. As Butler in her book *Self-Assertion for Women* states, setting limits is a way of teaching others how you like to be treated. You cannot assume that another person knows your needs and wants. People operate under different rules and values. It is up to you to let the other person know what is important to you.

Role play. Role play is an excellent way to rehearse a new behavior in a safe environment. Learning is more likely to take place. You can reenact an event with the client. Your client plays the role of other person involved, while you play the client's role. Later the roles are reversed. You can demonstrate all the above techniques through role play.

Summary of Session

"We have reviewed a number of strategies for dealing with chronic worry. They work only so far as you put them into practice. We have spoken of the importance of being assertive. When you do not assert yourself, you do not exercise whatever amount of control you have interpersonally. Yet control is an issue for you, as it is for every person with panic and phobias. The more you take charge of your life, the more confident you will feel.

"We discussed that taking care of one's own needs does not mean that you must step on other people's toes. Even if you cannot control others, the likelihood is much higher that you can get what you want when you express it. But more importantly, you will feel much better because you spoke up. We reviewed ways to be assertive, giving a direct message, using 'I' vs. 'you' statements, making a request, and teaching others how you want to be treated."

Feedback from Client

"What questions, aside from what you brought up earlier, do you have about what we reviewed today? Are there any related issues you wish to address?"

Difficulties You May Encounter

It Is Difficult to Convey All This Information Without "Lecturing"

Your client will obviously retain the material better if this information is imparted in a dialogue. After introducing a specific strategy, you may ask your client if he or she has tried something similar in the past. You might also ask him or her to describe in the beginning of the session examples of worries and nonassertiveness. Then you can weave the information in to show how the strategy might be implemented in the particular case.

If your client has agoraphobia, and your treatment will span over sixteen weeks, you can spread out the information over a couple more sessions.

Homework

The homework for session 11 is as follows:

1. Worksheet 1: Panic Frequency and Intensity.

2. Read session 10 in your book and bring up any questions or comments.

3. Continue to make entries in Worksheet 6: Core Belief Log.

4. If fear of panic continues: Continue seeking out interoceptive exposures and record them in Worksheet 8. Fill out a sample of Worksheet 4: Challenging Automatic Thoughts.

If agoraphobia is present:

5. Exposures (for the client to record on Worksheet 10 and you on Therapist Record 10T, under "Planned Exposures"). Record interoceptives in feared situations on Worksheet 8. This homework was probably set in the beginning of the session.

imaginary social or physical constraints. Other times it occurs for fear of panicking and having no one to rescue them. In contrast, by repeatedly *leaving according to a preset plan*, the person can become convinced that he or she is not trapped. While this is not possible in all situations, it can be done one way or another in the majority of situations. Exiting is especially useful in the beginning of treatment and should be planned if the client complains of entrapment. Once convinced that he or she is not trapped, the client can remain in the situation till the end of the activity, e.g., a movie.

3. **How to Cope with the Urge to Leave or "Escape"**
   Clients will escape at one time or another, no matter how carefully the exposure was planned. If this occurs, the person should stay in the situation a bit longer before leaving, because it is better that the client leaves after the anxiety is somewhat lowered. After escaping, the person should return as soon as possible, preferably a few minutes later, but at least by the next day. An escape without a repeat attempt soon afterwards may lead to an increase in fear.

4. **Returning to the Scene of the "Crime"**
   Encourage your client to go to the place where the first or worst panic occurred or to the situation of the worst fear. Otherwise the place will always loom as an overriding threat.

Cognitive Coping Techniques

1. **Using Worksheet 4: Challenging Automatic Thoughts**
   This worksheet is an excellent preparation for an exposure. Once the client has learned it very well, it can be done mentally when anticipating or being in a fearful situation.

2. **Being a Participant-Observer and Staying in the Here and Now**
   When a person asks "What if . . . happens?," he or she is projecting into the future. One of the golden rules in exposures is staying in the here and now. The client can ask "What is happening right now, at this very moment?" "Am I handling this very moment? Can I do it for another minute?"

3. **Perceived Control Versus Lack of Control**
   Clients often scrutinize their environment for ways in which they lack control, e.g., "There are too many people here," "I can't see the exit." Instead, the person can learn to look at the ways he or she *does* have control: "Even if there are lots of people here, I can still get around. These people are not bothering me. In fact, they seem friendly/neutral." "I know exactly in what direction the exits are, in case of a life-threatening emergency."

4. **Plan on How to Cope with Anxiety and Panic**
   The client can ask himself or herself, "If I have a panic while driving or standing in line, how will I handle it?" The client can prepare him or herself by rehearsing exactly what cognitive and behavioral strategies to apply. At times the only recourse is to just ride through the panic. Learning to use humor can also help.

5. **Testing Out Hypotheses via Behavioral Experiments**
   The person can predict in advance what will happen during the exposure

(preferably writing the prediction down) and later compare it with the outcome. The person gathers tangible evidence to challenge fearful automatic thoughts. Afterwards, the person asks himself or herself, "Did it happen? What actually took place? What is my explanation?" *Note that it is not helpful to test feelings of anxiety and panic* (which the client *is* very likely to experience) *but rather to test behavioral events.*

Feedback from Client

Difficulties You May Encounter

"I'm Not Willing to Live with Uncertainty and Risk."

A client who has a basic view that he or she is not willing to take risks can pose a challenge. One approach you may try is to show the client through Socratic questioning that he or she takes risks in many other areas of life. You can also explore the meaning of this view; it may cover up a greater fear, magical thinking, etc. Ultimately, there is no hope if the person aspires to achieve absolute certainty. If this frame of mind persists, the client may not be ready for therapy at this time.

Example of a vignette:

Client:	I'm not willing to live with uncertainty and risk. These exposures are too risky for me.
Therapist:	You are absolutely right. Of course, you take risks: While driving you might panic, your car could break down, you could get stuck in traffic, you could get into an accident; in an elevator you could get really anxious, the elevator could get stuck, an earthquake could hit while you are in it. Let's separate out anxiety and panic reactions for a moment. Do you think any of these involve imminent threats to your life each time?
Client:	No, but something *could* happen.
Therapist:	Very true, something could happen, because anything in life is possible. Our lives are filled with uncertainty. Do you think no person should drive, use elevators, or go to the store because of possible risks?
Client:	No, I wouldn't say that. I wouldn't go that far.
Therapist:	Good enough! Now, do you take any risks in life?
Client:	Yes, but a minimum.
Therapist:	Do you buy canned goods, eat in restaurants, go to work, rush in the mornings?
Client:	Yeah.
Therapist:	So you already take many risks. May I draw a conclusion? We take risks all the time because nothing in life is risk-free. Life is risk. Whatever we do or don't do, we'll die anyway. The dilemma really

is, do we want to always live in the shadow of death, or do we want to truly live while life lasts?

Client:	I'd rather try to enjoy life.
Therapist:	That's exactly what we are talking about! Leading a normal life involves going to stores, using elevators, driving. I'm only asking you to give your life a chance. As far as your death, like mine, I can't foresee the future.

"I'm Having a Bad Day. I Can't Do Exposures Today."

As a first step, explore what exactly this feeling is based on. Many clients experience this early in the morning. Here, your client can use behavioral approaches and cognitive techniques. One of the best behavioral approaches is to get up from bed immediately and get involved with the day's activities rather than try to analyze their feelings. This can be combined with thought stopping.

Example of a vignette:

Client:	Some days I wake up with the feeling it will be a bad day. I feel I can't do exposures then.
Therapist:	Can you tell me exactly what you mean by "having a bad day"?
Client:	I just have this anxious feeling, a sinking feeling. I feel vulnerable and know if I push it, I may have a panic attack.
Therapist:	Your conclusion is then not to do exposures. Let me ask you, do you think you'll learn more from doing exposures on "good" than on "bad" days?
Client:	Probably on bad days.
Therapist:	You're right. Also, what have you learned about subtle avoidance?
Client:	It's not good.
Therapist:	Do you know why?
Client:	You don't move forward.
Therapist:	That's right. Since your phobias started, have you often tried to take it easy on your "bad days"?
Client:	Yes.
Therapist:	Has it helped your phobias get better?
Client:	No.
Therapist:	That's right. It's like putting a band-aid on a big sore. It makes you feel good at the moment, but in the long run it does not help at all; it makes it worse. You know, this is like one of the many crossroads you face. Do you take a step forward or back? You have to look inside, and I know it must be a very lonely place inside facing all those fears. I cannot do that for you. But if you decide to move forward, I'll guide you and give you lots of support. What do you think?

Assume client chooses to move forward.

Therapist: Let's get to work. You need to overcome this vulnerability for "bad" days. One of the very best ways is to plan exposures early in the day every single day. Decide what you'll do, what time, and for how long. If you wake up feeling it's a bad day, do your exposure anyway.

If your client has no phobias or no phobias can be done daily early in the day, have him or her do interoceptives instead.

"I Can't Help It. I Step on the Brakes When I Go Too Fast."

Example of a vignette:

Client: I can't help it. I step on the brakes when I go too fast.

Therapist: How fast is too fast?

Client: Usually forty miles an hour.

Therapist: I assume you are not using freeways.

Client: No, but on major thoroughfares, especially going downhill. It really scares me.

Therapist: What are you afraid of?

Client: I won't be able to brake the car. It has nothing to do with my car's actual brakes. They are fine. It's me.

(It is exceedingly helpful here to accompany your client on an exposure. You might be able to help and guide your client. Let's assume your client frequently steps on the brakes without an external reason.)

Therapist: Can you work with a coach? For example, do you have someone willing to accompany you on a number of driving exposures?

Client: Yes, I have someone.

Therapist: Great. You might work with a coach, preferably someone who can work with you using rewards. You can practice driving on a major thoroughfare when there's very little traffic. Have your coach follow you in another car. Whenever you step on the brake without an external reason (which your coach can judge if the road is rather empty), your coach will make a note. The first time your coach's task is to just get a baseline. Then he or she and you will decide on rewards for using the brakes less than your baseline. For example, if your baseline is stepping on the brakes unnecessarily fifty times in thirty minutes, you could be rewarded initially for braking maximum thirty-five times in thirty minutes. This gets repeated, rewarding even fewer brake uses, until you no longer apply the brake without a reason. Such a plan is quite involved but also effective. I have had clients who did it with great success. What do you think? Are you willing to try?

Client: Yes.

Therapist: Good. We'll monitor this very closely.

Little Integration Between the Panic and Agoraphobia Work

You may consider asking your client to report how he or she is applying what has been learned in any given session to the phobic situations. If you do, remember to follow up on it when you review agoraphobic exposures in the following session. Example:

Therapist: I will ask you how you have applied what you learned in this session to phobic situations.

In the following session:

Therapist: Have you tried to apply what you learned in the last session to phobic situations? If so, how?

Worksheet 9: Goal and the Steps to Achieve It

Reward for Goal Achieved: _____

Goal No. _____

Date Achieved: _____

Currently able to do:

Date starting: _____

(Use all, some, or add circles, as needed).

Example: Goal and the Steps to Achieve It

Worksheet 9: Goal and the Steps to Achieve It

Reward for Goal Achieved: _Spouse pays membership in health spa._

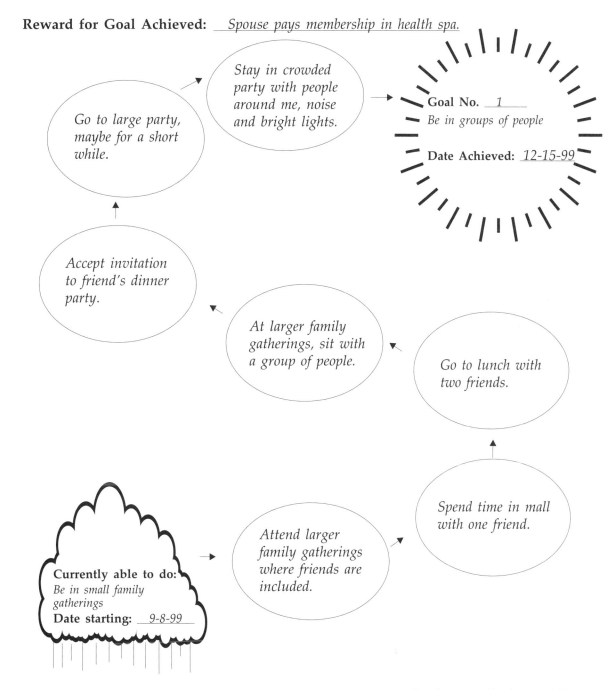

Go to large party, maybe for a short while.

Stay in crowded party with people around me, noise and bright lights.

Goal No. _1_
Be in groups of people

Date Achieved: _12-15-99_

Accept invitation to friend's dinner party.

At larger family gatherings, sit with a group of people.

Go to lunch with two friends.

Currently able to do:
Be in small family gatherings
Date starting: _9-8-99_

Attend larger family gatherings where friends are included.

Spend time in mall with one friend.

(Use all, some, or add circles, as needed.)

Therapist Record 9T:
Tracking Goal Progress

		Check if Progress Made on Goals															
Name	Goals	Treatment Weeks															
		1	2	3	4	5	6	7	8	9	10	11	12	13	14	15	16

Worksheet 10: Your Weekly Exposures

Goals: 1. _____   5. _____

               2. _____   6. _____

               3. _____   7. _____

               4. _____   8. _____

	Planned Exposures		Actual Effort	
Week Starting	Steps	Distance/ Time No. attempts per week	Steps	Distance/ Time No. attempts per week

For every step, record: Distance covered or Time, and Number of attempts per week.

Therapist Record 10T: Tracking Client's Weekly Exposures

Week Starting: _____

	Planned Exposures		Actual Effort	
Week Starting	Steps	Distance/ Time No. attempts per week	Steps	Distance/ Time No. attempts per week

Appendix

Treatment Plan

Problem: Panic and agoraphobia

Definition: Sudden panic symptoms that may include shortness of breath, hyperventilation, racing or pounding heart, hot flashes and sweating, dizziness, faint feelings, trembling, and muscle weakness. The severity of symptoms results in a fear of dying and/or losing control, and a persistent concern about experiencing additional attacks. Symptoms of agoraphobia include a fear and avoidance of environments or situations associated with panic.

Goals: Reduce the frequency and severity of panic attacks; reduce fear of panic; reduce agoraphobic avoidance.

Objectives:	Interventions:
1. Understanding the disorder.	1. Education regarding the physiology of fear and panic and the relationship between panic and avoidance.
2. Control hyperventilation.	2. Teach and practice diaphragmatic breathing.
3. Identify and change panic-building automatic thoughts.	3. Identify and challenge automatic thoughts occurring during panics; identify cognitive distortions; educate about focal fears (i.e., fainting, heart attack, etc.).
4. Identify and change core beliefs.	4. Introduce "unfolding the belief" technique and the Core Belief Log.

5. Overcome fear of physical panic symptoms.

6. Reduce phobic avoidance.

5. Introduce interoceptive exercises; desensitize to specific symptoms.

6. State goals regarding feared situations; step-by-step exposure.

Diagnosis: 300.01 Panic Disorder without Agoraphobia

300.21 Panic Disorder with Agoraphobia

References

American Psychiatric Association. 1994. *Diagnostic and Statistical Manual of Mental Disorders, Fourth Edition.* Washington, D.C.: American Psychiatric Association.

Argyle, N. 1988. "The Nature of Cognitions in Panic Disorder." *Behaviour Research and Therapy* 26(3):261-264.

Bandura, A. 1977. "Self-Efficacy: Toward a Unifying Theory of Behavioral Change." *Psychological Review* 84(2):191-215.

Bandura, A. 1988. "Self-Efficacy Conception of Anxiety." *Anxiety Research* 1:77-98.

Barlow, D.H. 1986. "Behavioral Conception and Treatment of Panic." *Psychopharmacology Bulletin* 22(3):802-806.

Barlow, D.H. 1988. *Anxiety and Its Disorders: The Nature and Treatment of Anxiety and Panic.* New York: The Guilford Press.

Barlow, D.H. 1990. "Long-Term Outcome for Patients With Panic Disorder Treated with Cognitive-Behavioral Therapy." *Journal of Clinical Psychiatry* 51(12, Suppl. A):17-23.

Barlow, D.H. 1997. "Cognitive-Behavioral Therapy for Panic Disorder: Current Status," and "Discussion: Cognitive-Behavioral Therapy." *Journal of Clinical Psychiatry* 58(Suppl. 2):32-37.

Barlow, D.H., and M.G. Craske. 1994. *Mastery of Your Anxiety and Panic II.* San Antonio, TX: Graywind Publications/The Psychological Corporation.

Barlow, D.H., M.G. Craske, J.A. Cerny, and J.S. Klosko. 1989. "Behavioral Treatment of Panic Disorder." *Behavior Therapy* 20:261-282.

Başoğlu, M. 1992. "Pharmacological and Behavioural Treatment of Panic Disorder." *Psychotherapy Psychosomatics* 58:57-59.

Beck, A.T., and G. Emery, with R.L. Greenberg. 1985. *Anxiety Disorders and Phobias: A Cognitive Perspective.* New York: Basic Books.

Beck, A.T., L. Sokol, D.A. Clark, R. Berchick, and F. Wright. 1992. "A Crossover Study of Focused Cognitive Therapy for Panic Disorder." *American Journal of Psychiatry* 149(6):778-783.

Beck, J.S. 1995. *Cognitive Therapy: Basics and Beyond.* New York: The Guilford Press.

Burns, D.D. 1989. *The Feeling Good Handbook.* New York: William Morrow & Co.

Butler, P.E. 1992. *Self-Assertion for Women.* San Francisco: Harper & Row Publishers.

Clark, D.B., B.E. Hirsch, M.G. Smith, J.M.R. Furman, and R.G. Jacob. 1994. "Panic in Otolaryngology Patients Presenting with Dizziness and Hearing Loss." *American Journal of Psychiatry* 151(8):1223-1225.

Clark, D.M. 1986. "A Cognitive Approach to Panic." *Behaviour Research and Therapy* 24(4):461-470.

Clark, D.M. and A. Ehlers. 1993. "An Overview of the Cognitive Theory and Treatment of Panic Disorder." *Applied and Preventive Psychology* 2:131-139.

Clark, D.M., P.M. Salkovskis, A. Hackmann, H. Middleton, P. Anastasiades, and M. Gelder. 1994. "A Comparison of Cognitive Therapy, Applied Relaxation and Imipramine in the Treatment of Panic Disorder." *British Journal of Psychiatry* 164:759-769.

Clum, G.A., S. Broyles, J. Borden, and P.L. Watkins. 1990. "Validity and Reliability of the Panic Attack Symptoms and Cognition Questionnaire." *Journal of Psychopathology and Behavioral Assessment* 12:233-245.

Craske, M.G. 1991. "Models and Treatment of Panic: Behavioral Therapy of Panic." *Journal of Cognitive Psychotherapy: An International Quarterly* 5(3):199-214.

Craske, M.G. and D.H. Barlow. 1994. *Agoraphobia Supplement to the Mastery of Your Anxiety and Panic II (MAP II Program).* San Antonio, TX: Graywind Publications/The Psychological Corporation.

Craske, M.G., T.A. Brown, and D.H. Barlow 1991. "Behavioral Treatment of Panic Disorder: A Two-Year Follow-up." *Behavior Therapy* 22:289-304.

Craske, M.G., E. Meadows, and D.H. Barlow. 1994. *Therapist's Guide for the Mastery of Your Anxiety and Panic II & Agoraphobia Supplement.* San Antonio, TX: Graywind Publications/The Psychological Corporation.

Craske, M.G., and B.I. Rodriguez 1994. "Behavioral Treatment of Panic Disorders and Agoraphobia." *Progress in Behavior Modification* 29:1-26.

Davis, M., E. Robbins-Eshelman, and M. McKay. 1995. *The Relaxation & Stress Reduction Workbook, Fourth Edition.* Oakland: New Harbinger Publications.

Dijkman-Caes, C.I.M., H.F. Kraan, and M.W. deVries. 1993. "Research on Panic Disorder and Agoraphobia in Daily Life: A Review of Current Studies." *Journal of Anxiety Disorders* 7:235-247.

Foa, E.B., and M.J. Kozak. 1986. "Emotional Processing of Fear: Exposure to Corrective Information." *Psychological Bulletin* 99(1):20-35.

Fyer, A.J., S. Mannuzza, and J.D. Coplan. 1995. "Anxiety Disorders." In: *Comprehensive Textbook of Psychiatry/VI.* Eds. H.I. Kaplan and B.J. Sadock. Baltimore: Williams and Wilkins.

Gerdes, T., W.R. Yates, and G. Clancy. 1995. "Increasing Identification and Referral of Panic Disorder Over the Past Decade." *Psychosomatics* 36(5):480-486.

Goisman, R.M., M.G. Warshaw, G.S. Steketee, E.J. Fierman, M.P. Rogers, I. Goldenberg, N.J. Weinshenker, R.G. Vasile, and M.B. Keller. 1995. "DSM-IV and the Disappearance of Agoraphobia Without a History of Panic Disorder: New Data on a Controversial Diagnosis." *American Journal of Psychiatry* 152(10):1438-1443.

Gould, R.A., M.W. Otto, and M.H. Pollack. 1995. "A Meta-Analysis of Treatment Outcome for Panic Disorder." *Clinical Psychology Review* 15(8):819-844.

Greenberger, D., and C.A. Padesky. 1995. *Mind Over Mood: A Cognitive Therapy Treatment Manual for Clients.* New York: The Guilford Press.

Hoffman, D.L., D.P. O'Leary, and D.J. Munjack. 1994. "Autorotation Test Abnormalities of the Horizontal and Vertical Vestibulo-Ocular Reflexes in Panic Disorder." *Otolaryngology—Head and Neck Surgery* 110(3):259-269.

Katerndahl, D.A., and J.P. Realini. 1995. "Where Do Panic Attack Sufferers Seek Care?" *Journal of Family Practice* 40(3):237-243.

Katon, W. 1989. *Panic Disorder in the Medical Setting.* National Institute of Mental Health, DHHS Pub. No.(ADM)89-1629. Washington, D.C.: Supt. of Docs., U.S. Govt. Print. Off.

Kessler, R.C., K.A. McGonagle, S. Zhao, C.B. Nelson, M. Hughes, S. Eshleman, H.-U. Wittchen, and K.S. Kendler. 1994. "Lifetime and 12-Month Prevalence of DSM-III-R Psychiatric Disorders in the United States: Results From the National Comorbidity Survey." *Archives of General Psychiatry* 51:8-19.

Kinney, P.J., and S.L. Williams. 1988. "Accuracy of Fear Inventories and Self-Efficacy Scales in Predicting Agoraphobic Behavior." *Behaviour Research and Therapy* 26(6):513-518.

Klein, D.F. 1993. "False Suffocation Alarms, Spontaneous Panics, and Related Conditions: An Integrative Hypothesis." *Archives of General Psychiatry* 50:306-317.

Klosko, J.S., D.H. Barlow, R. Tassinari, and J.A. Cerny, 1990. "A Comparison of Alprazolam and Behavior Therapy in Treatment of Panic Disorder." *Journal of Consulting and Clinical Psychology* 58(1):77-84.

Ley, R. 1985. "Blood, Breath, and Fears: A Hyperventilation Theory of Panic Attacks and Agoraphobia." *Clinical Psychology Review* 5:271-285.

Ley, R. 1988. "Panic Attacks During Sleep: A Hyperventilation-Probability Model." *Journal of Behavior Therapy and Experimental Psychiatry* 19(3):181-192.

Lidren, D.M., P.L. Watkins, R.A. Gould, G.A. Clum, M. Asterino, and H.L. Tulloch. 1994. "A Comparison of Bibliotherapy and Group Therapy in the Treatment of Panic Disorder." *Journal of Consulting and Clinical Psychology* 63(4):865-869.

Marchione, K.E., L. Michelson, M. Greenwald, and C. Dancu. 1987. "Cognitive Behavioral Treatment of Agoraphobia." *Behaviour Research and Therapy* 25(5):319-328.

Margraf, J., D.H. Barlow, D.M. Clark, and M.J. Telch. 1993. "Psychological Treatment of Panic: Work in Progress on Outcome, Active Ingredients, and Follow-up." *Behaviour Research and Therapy* 31(1):1-8.

Margraf, J., A. Ehlers, and W.T. Roth. 1986. "Biological Models of Panic Disorder and Agoraphobia—A Review." *Behaviour Research and Therapy* 24(5):553-567.

Marks, I.M. 1985. "Behavioral Psychotherapy for Anxiety Disorders." *Psychiatric Clinics of North America* 8(1):25-35.

Marks, I.M. 1987. "Behavioral Aspects of Panic Disorder." *American Journal of Psychiatry* 144(9):1160-1165.

Marks, I.M., R.P. Swinson, M. Başoğlu, K. Kuch, H. Noshirvani, G. O'Sullivan, P.T. Lelliott, M. Kirby, G. McNamee, S. Sengün, and K. Wickwire. 1993. "Alprazolam and Exposure Alone and Combined in Panic Disorder With Agoraphobia: A Controlled Study in London and Toronto." *British Journal of Psychiatry* 162:776-787.

McNally, R.J. 1990. "Psychological Approaches to Panic Disorder: A Review." *Psychological Bulletin* 108(3):403-419.

McNally, R.J. 1994. *Panic Disorder: A Critical Analysis.* New York: The Guilford Press.

Michelson, L.K. and K. Marchione. 1991. "Behavioral, Cognitive, and Pharmacological Treatments of Panic Disorder With Agoraphobia: Critique and Synthesis." *Journal of Consulting and Clinical Psychology* 59(1):100-114.

Otto, M.W. 1997. "Integrated Treatment of Panic Disorder." Pp. 40-42 In: "Panic Disorder: A Treatment Update." *Journal of Clinical Psychiatry* 58:36-42.

Padesky, C.A. 1994. "Schema Change Processes in Cognitive Therapy." *Clinical Psychology and Psychotherapy* 1(5):267-278.

Persons, J.B. 1989. *Cognitive Therapy in Practice: A Case Formulation Approach.* New York: W.W. Norton and Company.

Reiss, S. 1987. "Theoretical Perspectives on the Fear of Anxiety." *Clinical Psychology Review* 7:585-596.

Reiss, S., R.A. Peterson, D.M. Gursky, and R.J. McNally. 1986. "Anxiety Sensitivity, Anxiety Frequency and the Prediction of Fearfulness." *Behaviour Research and Therapy* 24(1):1-8.

Seligman, M.E.P. 1990. *Learned Optimism.* New York: Pocket Books.

Sobel, D.S., and Ornstein, R. 1996. *The Healthy Mind, Healthy Body Handbook.* Los Altos, Calif.: DRX.

Telch, M.J., N.B. Schmidt, T.L. Jaimez, K.M. Jacquin, and P.J. Harrington. 1995. "Impact of Cognitive-Behavioral Treatment on Quality of Life in Panic Disorder Patients." *Journal of Consulting and Clinical Psychology* 63(5):823-830.

Treatment of Panic Disorder. 1991. *NIH Consensus Development Conference, Consensus Statement.* Sept. 25-27, 9(2).

van den Hout, M., A. Arntz, and R. Hoekstra. 1994. "Exposure Reduced Agoraphobia but Not Panic, and Cognitive Therapy Reduced Panic but Not Agoraphobia." *Behaviour Research and Therapy* 32(4):447-451.

Williams, S.L. 1982. *Comparative Power of Guided Mastery and Exposure Treatments for Intractable Phobias.* Doctoral dissertation, Stanford University, Stanford, Calif.

Williams, S.L. 1985. "On the Nature and Measurement of Agoraphobia." *Progress in Behavior Modification* 19:109-144.

Williams, S.L. 1987. "On Anxiety and Phobia." *Journal of Anxiety Disorders* 1:161-180.

Williams, S.L. 1990. "Guided Mastery Treatment of Agoraphobia: Beyond Stimulus Exposure." *Progress in Behavior Modification* 26:89-121.

Williams, S.L. 1992. "Perceived Self-Efficacy and Phobic Disability." In: *Self-Efficacy: Thought Control of Action.* Ed. R. Schwarzer. Washington, D.C.: Hemisphere.

Williams, S.L., G. Dooseman, and E. Kleifield. 1984. "Comparative Effectiveness of Guided Mastery and Exposure Treatments for Intractable Phobias." *Journal of Consulting and Clinical Psychology* 52(4):505-518.

Williams, S.L., and B. Laberge. 1994. "Panic Disorder with Agoraphobia." In: *Adult Behavior Therapy Casebook.* Eds. C.G. Last and M. Hersen. New York: Plenum Press.

Williams, S. L., and G. Zane. 1989. "Guided Mastery and Stimulus Exposure Treatments for Severe Performance Anxiety in Agoraphobics." *Behaviour Research and Therapy* 27(3):237-245.

Woods, S.W., D.H. Barlow, J.H. Gorman, and M.K. Shear. 1998. "Follow-up Results Six Months After Discontinuation of All Treatment." In: *Results From the Multi-Center Clinical Trial on the Treatment of Panic Disorder: Cognitive Behavior Treatment Versus Imipramine Versus Their Combination.* Chair, D.H. Barlow. Symposium presented at the 32nd Annual convention of the Association for Advancement of Behavior Therapy, Washington, D.C.

Zarate, R., and W.S. Agras. 1994. "Psychosocial Treatment of Phobia and Panic Disorders." *Psychiatry* 57:133-141.

Zuercher-White, E. 1997. *Treating Panic Disorder and Agoraphobia: A Step-by-Step Clinical Guide.* Oakland: New Harbinger Publications.

Best Practices for Therapy

Each of the protocols in this series presents a session-by-session, research-based treatment plan, including evaluation instruments, sample treatment summaries for use with managed care, handouts, weekly homework, and strategies to use for delivering key information. Each is accompanied by its own client manual, containing all the materials that the client will need.

Additional Titles Now Available

OVERCOMING OBSESSIVE-COMPULSIVE DISORDER
A 14-session treatment. By Gail Steketee, Ph.D.
Therapist Protocol. *Item OCDP $24.95*
Client manual. *Item OCDM $11.95*
Client Pack. Set of five client manuals. *Item OCM5 29.95*

OVERCOMING POST-TRAUMATIC STRESS DISORDER
An 11- to 24-session treatment. By Larry Smyth, Ph.D.
Therapist Protocol. *Item PTSP $24.95*
Client manual. *Item PTSM $11.95*
Client Pack. Set of five client manuals. *Item PTM5 29.95*

OVERCOMING SPECIFIC PHOBIA
A 10-session treatment. By Edmund J. Bourne, Ph.D.
Therapist Protocol. *Item POSP $19.95*
Client Manual. *Item PHM $9.95*
Client Pack. Set of five client manuals. *Item PHM5 $24.95*

In Preparation

Overcoming Borderline Personality Disorder
Overcoming Generalized Anxiety Disorder
Overcoming Anger
Overcoming Depression
Overcoming Social Phobia

Call toll-free 1-800-748-6273 to order. Have your Visa or Mastercard number ready. Or send a check for the titles you want to New Harbinger Publications, 5674 Shattuck Avenue, Oakland, CA 94609. Include $3.80 for the first item and 75¢ for each additional item to cover shipping and handling. (California residents please include appropriate sales tax.) Allow four to six weeks for delivery.

Prices subject to change without notice.

Some Other New Harbinger Self-Help Titles

Claiming Your Creative Self: True Stories from the Everyday Lives of Women, $15.95
Six Keys to Creating the Life You Desire, $19.95
Taking Control of TMJ, $13.95
What You Need to Know About Alzheimer's, $15.95
Winning Against Relapse: A Workbook of Action Plans for Recurring Health and Emotional Problems, $14.95
Facing 30: Women Talk About Constructing a Real Life and Other Scary Rites of Passage, $12.95
The Worry Control Workbook, $15.95
Wanting What You Have: A Self-Discovery Workbook, $18.95
When Perfect Isn't Good Enough: Strategies for Coping with Perfectionism, $13.95
The Endometriosis Survival Guide, $13.95
Earning Your Own Respect: A Handbook of Personal Responsibility, $12.95
High on Stress: A Woman's Guide to Optimizing the Stress in Her Life, $13.95
Infidelity: A Survival Guide, $13.95
Stop Walking on Eggshells, $14.95
Consumer's Guide to Psychiatric Drugs, $16.95
The Fibromyalgia Advocate: Getting the Support You Need to Cope with Fibromyalgia and Myofascial Pain, $18.95
Healing Fear: New Approaches to Overcoming Anxiety, $16.95
Working Anger: Preventing and Resolving Conflict on the Job, $12.95
Sex Smart: How Your Childhood Shaped Your Sexual Life and What to Do About It, $14.95
You Can Free Yourself From Alcohol & Drugs, $13.95
Amongst Ourselves: A Self-Help Guide to Living with Dissociative Identity Disorder, $14.95
Healthy Living with Diabetes, $13.95
Dr. Carl Robinson's Basic Baby Care, $10.95
Better Boundries: Owning and Treasuring Your Life, $13.95
Goodbye Good Girl, $12.95
Being, Belonging, Doing, $10.95
Thoughts & Feelings, Second Edition, $18.95
Depression: How It Happens, How It's Healed, $14.95
Trust After Trauma, $15.95
The Chemotherapy & Radiation Survival Guide, Second Edition, $14.95
Surviving Childhood Cancer, $12.95
The Headache & Neck Pain Workbook, $14.95
Perimenopause, $16.95
The Self-Forgiveness Handbook, $12.95
A Woman's Guide to Overcoming Sexual Fear and Pain, $14.95
Don't Take It Personally, $12.95
Becoming a Wise Parent For Your Grown Child, $12.95
Clear Your Past, Change Your Future, $13.95
Preparing for Surgery, $17.95
The Power of Two, $15.95
It's Not OK Anymore, $13.95
The Daily Relaxer, $12.95
The Body Image Workbook, $17.95
Living with ADD, $17.95
When Anger Hurts Your Kids, $12.95
The Chronic Pain Control Workbook, Second Edition, $17.95
Fibromyalgia & Chronic Myofascial Pain Syndrome, $19.95
Kid Cooperation: How to Stop Yelling, Nagging & Pleading and Get Kids to Cooperate, $13.95
The Stop Smoking Workbook: Your Guide to Healthy Quitting, $17.95
Conquering Carpal Tunnel Syndrome and Other Repetitive Strain Injuries, $17.95
An End to Panic: Breakthrough Techniques for Overcoming Panic Disorder, Second Edition, $18.95
Letting Go of Anger: The 10 Most Common Anger Styles and What to Do About Them, $12.95
Messages: The Communication Skills Workbook, Second Edition, $15.95
Coping With Chronic Fatigue Syndrome: Nine Things You Can Do, $13.95
The Anxiety & Phobia Workbook, Second Edition, $18.95
The Relaxation & Stress Reduction Workbook, Fourth Edition, $17.95
Living Without Depression & Manic Depression: A Workbook for Maintaining Mood Stability, $18.95
Coping With Schizophrenia: A Guide For Families, $15.95
Visualization for Change, Second Edition, $15.95
Angry All the Time: An Emergency Guide to Anger Control, $12.95
Couple Skills: Making Your Relationship Work, $14.95
Self-Esteem, Second Edition, $13.95
I Can't Get Over It, A Handbook for Trauma Survivors, Second Edition, $16.95
Dying of Embarrassment: Help for Social Anxiety and Social Phobia, $13.95
The Depression Workbook: Living With Depression and Manic Depression, $17.95
Men & Grief: A Guide for Men Surviving the Death of a Loved One, $14.95
When Once Is Not Enough: Help for Obsessive Compulsives, $14.95
Beyond Grief: A Guide for Recovering from the Death of a Loved One, $14.95
Hypnosis for Change: A Manual of Proven Techniques, Third Edition, $15.95
When Anger Hurts, $13.95

Call **toll free, 1-800-748-6273,** to order. Have your Visa or Mastercard number ready. Or send a check for the titles you want to New Harbinger Publications, Inc., 5674 Shattuck Ave., Oakland, CA 94609. Include $3.80 for the first book and 75¢ for each additional book, to cover shipping and handling. (California residents please include appropriate sales tax.) Allow two to five weeks for delivery.

Prices subject to change without notice.